Scarlet Macaws

All rights reserved. No part of this publication may be reproduced or transmitted in any form or by any means, electronic or mechanical, including photocopying, recording, or by any information storage or retrieval system, without the prior written permission of the copyright owner and the publisher.

This publication is Copyright 2013 by EKL Publishing. All products, publications, software and services mentioned and recommended in this publication are protected by trademarks. In such instance, all trademarks & copyright belong to the respective owners.

The moral rights of the author has been asserted

British Library Cataloguing in Publication Data

A catalogue record for this book is available from the British Library

ISBN 978–1–909820–25–8

Disclaimer and Legal Notice

While every attempt has been made to verify the information shared in this publication, neither shall the author nor publisher assume any responsibility for errors, omissions, nor contrary interpretation of the subject matter herein. Any perceived slight to any specific person(s) or organisation(s) are purely unintentional. You need to do your own due diligence to determine if the content of this product is correct for you.

This book is presented solely for educational and entertainment purposes. The author and publisher are not offering it as legal, accounting, or other professional services advice. While best efforts have been used in preparing this book, the author, affiliates and publisher make no representations or warranties of any kind and assume no liabilities of any kind with respect to the accuracy or completeness of the contents and specifically disclaim any implied warranties of merchantability or fitness of use for a particular purpose. Neither shall the author nor the publisher be held liable or responsible to any person or entity with respect to any loss or incidental or consequential damages caused, or alleged to have been caused, directly or indirectly, by the information or programs contained herein. The author shall not be liable for any loss incurred as a consequence of the use and application, direct or indirectly, of any information presented in this work. This publication is designed to provide information in regard to the subject matter covered. It is the reader's responsibility to find advice before putting anything written in the book into practice.

References are provided for informational purposes only and do not constitute endorsement of any websites or other sources. Readers should be aware that the websites listed in this book may change. We have no control over the nature, content, and availability of the websites listed in this book. The inclusion of any website links does not necessarily imply a recommendation or endorse the views expressed within them. EKL Publishing takes no responsibility for, and will not be liable for, the website being temporally unavailable or being removed from the internet. The information in this book is not intended to serve as legal advice.

Scarlet Macaws

The Complete Owner's Guide

Information and Facts on Scarlet Macaws
Including Health, Diet, Cages, Temperament,
Lifespan, Personality, Breeders and
Suitability as Pets

Foreword

Hello and thank you for buying my book.

In this book you will find some wonderful information to help you care for your Scarlet Macaw. I've included in this book information about their personality, temperament habitat, cages, diet, facts, set up, food, life span, breeding, feeding costs and a care sheet.

I have written this book using American spelling as that is what I'm used to. I have given measurements in both feet and inches/pounds and ounces and also in metric. I have also given costs in US$ and GBP. Both the measurements and costs are approximate guides. I have done my best to ensure the accuracy of the information in this book as at the time of publication.

I trust that after reading this book you will enjoy the experience of owning and looking after a Scarlet Macaw and that you have a wonderful time enjoying the pleasure they bring in the years to come!

All good wishes,

Rose Sullivan

Acknowledgments

A Scarlet Macaw is a truly magnificent bird and I must thank my dear friend Sue for introducing me to her gorgeous pal Azora who is one of the most inquisitive and engaging birds I've ever met.

Sue has given me her insights and experiences and helped me with the contents of this book along with some great feedback. Azora made her own contribution too by giving me an excited welcome every time I called.

I must also thank my husband Marc and our children Mike and Cathy for their love and patience as I end up spending most evenings working in front of the computer. Their understanding and love for my passion makes the whole journey worthwhile.

Table of Contents

Commonly Used Terms 1
Chapter 1: Introduction 4
   Companion Birds 7
   History of the Parrot Society of the UK 9
   History of the North American Parrot Society 9
Chapter 2: Origins and Characteristics 11
    The Illegal Parrot Trade 12
    Feeding Habits in the Wild 13
   Physical Characteristics 13
     Size and Weight 14
     Beak 14
     Vivid Coloration 15
     Loud Vocalizations 16
   Mating and Breeding 16
     Care of the Young 18
     Defense of the Nest 18
   Unusual Longevity for a Pet 18
   Your Macaw and Your Will 19
Chapter 3: Scarlet Macaws as Pets 21
   What to Know Before You Buy 22
     Human Health Considerations 22
     Macaws Live a Long Time 23
     Macaws Have Emotional Needs 23

- On-going Socialization 24
- Time outside the Cage 24
- Aggressive Chewing 25
- Loud Squawking 25
- Other Pets and Children 26
- Daily Maintenance 27
- What about Wing Clipping? 28
- Tips for Buying a Scarlet Macaw 30
  - More than One? 32
  - Male or Female? 32
  - Judge the Bird's Demeanor 33
  - Handle the Macaw 33
  - Request a Vet Exam 33
  - Expect to Answer Questions 34
  - The Bird's Welfare Comes First 34
- Costs and Other Considerations 35
  - Projected Costs 35
  - Ongoing Overheads 38
- Aviaries 39
  - Aviaries and Breeders in the U.S.A. 40
  - Aviaries and Breeders in the U.K. 48
- Pros and Cons of Owning a Scarlet Macaw 49
- Chapter 4: Bird Proofing Your Home 51
- Chapter 5: Home Sweet Home 58
  - Picking the Perfect Cage 59

Important Cage Features	59
Be Cautious About Materials	60
Cage Costs	61
Cage Placement	61
Cage Maintenance	62
An Outdoor Option?	64
Use a Double Door Design	64
Plans and Ideas Online	65
Macaws Love Playgrounds	66
Toys, Toys and More Toys	67

Chapter 6: Daily Care 69

Diet and Nutrition	70
Treats	72
Food and Water Dispensers	73
Mineral Block	74
Chew Toys	74
Sleeping	75
Grooming and Bath Time	77
Nail Clipping	78
Tricks and Speech	80
Tips for Teaching Tricks	82
Understanding Scarlet Macaw Behavior	82
Handling Your Macaw	83
Using a Bird Harness	85
Travel Carrier	86

Time Away from Your Parrot 87
Coming Home Again 89
Chapter 7: Quick Facts on Behavior 90
Problem Behaviors 91
Learn to Read Body Language 92
Don't Retaliate 93
Push Back Appropriately 93
Preening 94
Other Common Behaviors 95
Chapter 8: Health 97
Signs of a Sick Bird 98
Common Health Issues 100
Chlamydiosis 100
Diarrhea 101
Feather Plucking 102
Arthritis in Older Birds 103
Scaly Face and Leg Disease 104
Aspergillosis 105
Candidiasis 105
Pacheco's Disease 105
Proventricular Dilation Disease (PDD) 106
Parrot Allergies in Humans 106
Dander Pneumoconiosis 107
Special Note: Avian Flu 108
Chapter 9: Veterinary Care 110

- Finding a Vet 111
- Interview Potential Avian Vets 113
- What happens in an emergency? 115
- Typical vets costs each year 116
- Annual Exam 117
- Pet Insurance 117

Chapter 10: Scarlet Macaw Care Sheet 121
- Housing and Habitat 122
  - Positioning the Cage 122
  - Cage Maintenance 123
- Chew Toys 124
- Diet and Nutrition 124
  - Food and Water Bowls 127
  - Mineral Supplementation 127
- Grooming 127
- Interaction and Training 127
- Bird Harnesses 128
- Free Flight Time 129

Chapter 11: Introduction to Breeding 130
- Basic Reproductive Facts 131
- Mate for Life 131
- Helpless Chicks 132
- Establishing a Breeding Pair 132
- Large Enclosure Required 134
- Final Observations 134

Chapter 12: Life after You 136
    Finding a Permanent Home for Your Macaw 139
    Making it Legal 141
Chapter 13: Closing Thoughts 142
Chapter 14: Frequently Asked Questions 146
Chapter 15: Relevant Websites 152
    Shopping 152
CITES and Parrots 155
References 160
Glossary 162
Index 166
Photo Credits 171

Commonly Used Terms

aviary – An aviary is an outdoor enclosure used for companion birds. Especially with a large species like the Scarlet Macaw, it is essential to provide adequate room for free flight in a safe environment. Aviaries must be secure and you must be able to safely transport the bird into your home during inclement weather.

aviculture – The practice of keeping a bird or birds as a companion, along with all the necessary equipment and tasks to provide for their physical and emotional needs is referred to as "aviculture."

beak – The upper and lower jaws or mandibles of a bird come together to form the beak. In Scarlet Macaws, the upper jaw is horn colored while the lower is black. They have the typical hooked beak present in most parrots, which they use in the wild to break open nuts and seeds.

cage – The indoor habitat used most commonly with companion birds is a cage commensurate with their size. Since Scarlet Macaws are one of the largest of the parrots, they require the biggest cage you can afford and house. Additionally, the birds need at least 2 hours of free flight time per day.

companion birds – Birds that live in close relationship with humans as pets are referred to as companion birds. Scarlet

Commonly Used Terms

Macaws are especially popular in this regard for their affectionate natures and high level of intelligence.

crop – When a bird consumes food, the material passes first to the crop, which is an organ much like a sac. It is responsible for a primary level of digestion. The crop is located between the esophagus and the stomach, and is clearly visible in chicks before their feathers come in. A full crop makes a bulge on a bird's upper breast.

cuttlebone – Cuttlebones are chew toys with the consistency of pumice that help a bird to keep its beak worn down while also providing a source of calcium.

feather – Feathers are flat structures of varying lengths that make up the plumage or body covering of a bird. The longest of these sit on the wings and tail.

free flying – Free flying is that period of time when a companion bird is allowed outside of its enclosure for exercise and pleasure. Scarlet Macaws need at least two hours of free flying per day to remain happy and healthy.

parrot – A parrot is any bird that is a member of the family Psittacidae. They are typically tropical in origin, brightly colored, and equipped with short, hooked beaks. Scarlet Macaws are one of the largest of the parrots, and are capable of mimicking human speech and other sounds.

veterinarian – Veterinarians are medical professionals that specialize in the regular and emergency medical needs of companion animals and livestock. You will need to locate an avian veterinarian with experience working with birds

Commonly Used Terms

to provide the optimum level of care for your Scarlet Macaw. Veterinarians are often referred to as vets.

zoonotic – Any disease that can be passed from an animal to a human is referred to as zoonotic. Please refer to the Chapter eight on Scarlet Macaw Health for a full discussion of this topic.

Chapter 1: Introduction

When most people hear the word "pet," they make the natural assumption that the speaker shares his or her home with a companion dog or cat. Most are surprised to hear that parrots, including the Scarlet Macaw, are not far behind these perennial favorites in terms of numbers.

Chapter 1: Introduction

Estimates suggest that there are as many as 40 million parrots living in households in the United States of America alone, with as many or more kept as companions in Europe.

These magnificent tropical birds that come in a huge range of colors and sizes are popular pets for many reasons, not the least of which is their natural intelligence.

Experts say that most parrots think on the same level as that of a 3 to 5 year old child. Since many varieties of these birds are long lived — Scarlet Macaws are known to reach 75 years of age — they assimilate an impressive body of information over their lifetimes.

Scarlet Macaws also referred to as Red–and–Yellow, Red–breasted or Red–Yellow–and–Blue Macaws. People speak lovingly of their companion Scarlet Macaws that can judge their human's moods and respond with both compassion and concern. One of the largest of the parrots, the Scarlet Macaw is also one of the most affectionate. You'll often see them described as "cuddly" and have a most engaging personality.

They are capable of learning words and phrases, often quite spontaneously, and are receptive to picking up "tricks." In a large part this is because "training" means more time with their person.

In the wild, Scarlet Macaws are monogamous and mate for life. When kept singly as pets, the bird will develop the same deep bond with their human, and will require attention and affection in return.

Chapter 1: Introduction

It is imperative to understand that a parrot has both physical and emotional needs. For many people, all the factors of parrot ownership are just too much. They include:–

- longevity
- psychological needs
- noise level
- daily cage maintenance

Unfortunately, in all too many cases, this realization comes too late. In the United States, the problem of unwanted companion parrots has become so serious that the Humane Society recommends the birds be euthanized.

Before you make a decision that will affect your life and that of a highly intelligent creature, you have a responsibility to do exactly what you are here to do, learn everything you can about what is involved in living with a parrot.

This book will give you practical information in an easily digestible form, but I would also like to recommend Joanna Burger's book "The Parrot Who Owns Me: The Story of a Relationship."

Burger, an animal behaviorist, adopted a Red–Lored Amazon Parrot named Tiko. The bird was already 30 years old, and had been badly neglected. Her narrative illustrates the incredibly complex relationship that can develop between a human and a bird, and fully explores the challenges of cross–species communication.

I highly recommend this excellent memoir of friendship between a human and a parrot for anyone considering adopting one of these remarkable creatures.

The Red Lored Amazon is about half the size of a Scarlet Macaw. When you read about life with Tiko, double everything! Are you up to the challenges of such a relationship?

If you are, having a Scarlet Macaw in your life will change you forever. Depending on your age, your bird could literally be with you for the rest of your life.

Given the serious implications for you and for the bird, weigh your decision thoroughly and only proceed when you're sure you're ready for the commitment. Anything less isn't fair to you, your loved ones or this magnificent parrot.

Companion Birds

Birds have been endeared as pets throughout the centuries, dating back as far as the ancient Egyptians, who shared their love of their feathered friends in their hieroglyphics. Literature discussing birds as pets first appeared in China in the third century AD. The love of large birds, such as parrots, has grown from century to century and from generation to generation.

Chapter 1: Introduction

The Scarlet Macaw is a wonderful example of the long history birds have as a companion to man and has been identified as having a place in the lives of the Incas dating back to the early 1100's. This magnificent specimen was formally recognized as the national symbol of Honduras in 1993 though sadly it is rare enough in the country due to continuing widespread poaching.

In the United States, parrots of all types became popular first pets in the White House. President Theodore Roosevelt, who held America's highest office from 1901 through 1909, shared the White House with a Blue and Gold Macaw and a Hyacinth Macaw.

In the United Kingdom, a gregarious and talkative Blue and Yellow Macaw named Charlie became the pet companion to Winston Churchill during World War II. Rumor has persisted through the decades that Charlie, a female, had a penchant for cursing Adolf Hitler and the Nazis.

Parrots became, both in the United States of America and in the United Kingdom, more popular as pets in the late 1960s and into the 1970s.

The increasing popularity of birds as pets more than five decades ago led to the creation of bird clubs, the emergence of rescue groups to care for birds of all sizes that find themselves homeless, the emergence and development of an avian veterinary industry, and an entire avian-related publishing industry (books, magazines and later online).

Chapter 1: Introduction

History of the Parrot Society of the UK

The Parrot Society of the UK, an international society that dates back to 1966, provides parrot owners – from those with tiny budgies to the much larger macaws – with a vast resource of information on their companion birds, hosts the premier parrot show in the United Kingdom, and brings parrots lovers together from around the world.

When the first meeting of the Parrot Society of the UK convened in 1966, little did its members know that within five decades the organization would boast more than 5,500 members in the United Kingdom and abroad.

The first issue of the organization's first magazine, Bird Scene, was published in 1967. Meetings of society members are still held throughout the United Kingdom on a regular basis.

To learn more about the Parrot Society of the UK, check out the website which features hundreds of links, information on membership, and even a junior section for budding parrot lovers at: www.theparrotsocietyuk.org

History of the North American Parrot Society

The North American Parrot Society, which first debuted in 1991, spans the whole of the United States and Canada with affiliated clubs scattered throughout both countries. The society has dual purposes: To educate parrot owners and potential parrot owners on how to best care for birds and to

Chapter 1: Introduction

make showing parrots at bird shows a safe and fun hobby for bird enthusiasts.

The North American Parrot Society participates in nearly two dozen shows and exhibits throughout the United States and Puerto Rico each year, educating bird owners and sharing in their passion for parrots of all sizes.

Membership to the North American Parrot Society is open to all parrot owners, regardless of whether they show their birds. Membership includes bird owners, avian veterinarians and breeders. Learn more about the North American Parrot Society by visiting the official website at: www.northamericanparrotsociety.com

Chapter 2: Origins and Characteristics

The Scarlet Macaw (Ara macao) is one of the largest of the world's parrots, and enjoys an unusually extensive range in the wild. These handsome and colorful birds live from south eastern Mexico into Peru, Honduras, Boliva and Brazil. They can also be found on the islands of Trinidad and Coiba but the greatest concentration lives in the Amazon basin.

Although they are threatened in their native regions by the destruction of their habitat, and as a consequence of the pet trade, Scarlet Macaws are listed in Appendix I of CITES, but classified by the International Union for Conservation of Nature (IUCN) as "least concern."

In part, this is because the Scarlet Macaw's native habitat covers approximately 6,700,000 km2. Even over that huge area, however, wild populations of the birds now vary widely in concentration.

Thankfully, enthusiasts breed Scarlet Macaws in captivity in large numbers, a fact that is saving these birds from the fate of so many rain forest animals.

Even though we trust that the vast majority of Scarlet Macaws we buy as pets today are captive bred and completely legal, it's important for parrot lovers to be aware of the illegal trade in this and other species.

The Illegal Parrot Trade

As an example, in Costa Rica baby Scarlet Macaws are stolen from their nests and sold for $200 / £130 each, only to be smuggled into the Unites States and other countries where they can command far higher prices.

When you begin to look for your own bird, it's important to work with reputable breeders who maintain active aviaries. Be cautious of anyone who has a single bird for sale. Try to find out the parrot's origin before making a purchase. Your desire is to support the species, not the illegal trade in exotic animals.

If you are interested in actively supporting the conservation of Scarlet Macaws and other parrot species in the wild, see the World Parrot Trust's website at www.parrots.org.

Feeding Habits in the Wild

Scarlet Macaws live in tall, deciduous trees — preferably near rivers — and like to be part of large groups. They exist on a diet of nuts, berries, seeds and leaves. Sometimes nectar and flowers are eaten as well.

Hardy by nature, they still protect themselves from potentially toxic plants by eating large amounts of clay, which acts as a neutralizing agent. In captivity, however, Scarlet Macaws don't require clay because their diets are supervised.

Typically, a Scarlet Macaw will use its left foot to hold and handle its food, using the right foot to support its body. The left foot works in concert with the beak, and this systematic approach gives the birds an unusual degree of dexterity.

Physical Characteristics

There are two subspecies that differ visibly by the width of the yellow band on the wing. These are Ara macao macao, the South American Scarlet Macaw, and Ara macao cyanoptera, the North Central American Scarlet Macaw.

Chapter 2: Origins and Characteristics

Size and Weight

A typical Scarlet Macaw measures 32 inches (81.3 cm) in length with their impressive tails accounting for better than half of that. No other species of parrot has a longer tail. The average weight is 2 to 3 pounds (907 to 1,361 grams).

Beak

The Scarlet Macaw has a prominent and highly useful beak that is pale or horn color on top and black on its lower half. It is hinged against the skull for independent movement, which increases its strength and flexibility .This structure looks powerful, because it is. Although pet Scarlet Macaws rarely bite, they're more than capable of doing so! The male has slightly larger bill.

Chapter 2: Origins and Characteristics

The beak is beautifully adapted for the bird's use in breaking into hard nuts, but macaws can also take tough seeds between their tongue and palate and grind them into a more digestible paste. They are also noted for using their beak as an extra limb to assist them in climbing.

Vivid Coloration

As you would expect, most of the Scarlet Macaw's feathers are vivid red. In spite of their colorful appearance, Macaws can remain well camouflaged in the rain forest canopy.

The rump and tail are a soft blue, with darker shades on the outermost flight feathers of the wings. Portions of the tail exhibit a deep red, with golden iridescence.

It is not unusual for some green to appear on the wings as well, but on the North Central American Scarlet Macaw, the green shading is dominant.

Around the macaw's eye, there is a patch of bare white skin. This soft, wrinkled area that extends toward the bill is completely free of feathers, and creamy in appearance.

Juvenile Scarlet Macaws have dark eyes. As the bird gets older, however, the eyes are light yellow and alight with keen intelligence and interest.

It is easy to confuse the Scarlet Macaw with the Green-Winged Macaw, but the latter has distinctive red facial lines and no yellow on the wings.

Loud Vocalizations

Scarlet Macaws are not quiet birds. They make their presence known! Sometimes a macaw will let loose with a high-pitched screech, and at others you'll hear a kind of low, throaty purr.

In captivity, macaws screech when they are trying to get their human's attention or communicate displeasure. "HEY! Where's my supper?"

Because macaws love routine, and seem to be perfectly capable of telling time, you can expect your pet to let you know if you're deviating from his perceived schedule. Never mind what's going on in your life!

If you've had a hard day at work, and your macaw senses your "down" mood, don't be surprised if your bird perches on your shoulder and coos in your ear.

Scarlet Macaws are well attuned to the well-being of their "mate" and are capable of expressing deep and genuine empathy.

Mating and Breeding

Scarlet Macaws reach sexual maturity at 3 to 4 years of age. They choose a single mate and remain monogamous for life. They breed one or two times per year, with the females laying 2 to 4 eggs that are white and rounded. The incubation period is 24 to 25 days.

Chapter 2: Origins and Characteristics

Mated Scarlet Macaws make affectionate couples. They will preen one another and lick each other's faces. Although the flock will gather as a group to sleep at night, mates spend their days flying and foraging together. The birds make their nests in hollowed portions of trees high in the canopy.

The only time mates are really alone is when the female is incubating the eggs and the male forages for food, which he brings back to feed to her.

Care of the Young

Hatchlings will remain with their parents for up to two years. Both parents participate in the rearing. The males will regurgitate liquefied food and feed the young in tandem with the female. The pair will not raise another "family" until their present offspring have become functionally independent.

Defense of the Nest

As confirmed previously, in spite of their colorful appearance, Macaws can remain well camouflaged in the canopy but will quietly leave their nests and sacrifice their eggs when threatened. Their main threats come from toucans, snakes, monkeys and large mammals. As adults, Scarlet Macaws can normally escape predation because of their size and their ability to fly.

Young birds in the nest are vulnerable, however, and even adults can be taken by large jungle cats including the jaguar. Eagles and hawks are also a serious threat.

Unusual Longevity for a Pet

It is not unusual for a Scarlet Macaw to reach an age of 75 years in captivity. If you're thinking about adopting a parrot, you may need to consider your age much more than that of your potential companion!

Chapter 2: Origins and Characteristics

It's highly likely that your bird will outlive you. It's quite common for parrot owners to make provisions in their wills for their pets.

Your Macaw and Your Will

If you are new to having a companion bird, including the animal in your will may seem downright silly – until you do the math. If you're 30 now, your bird could be with you until you're 105!

You might both make it, but in general, it's wiser to find someone who is willing to inherit the care of your macaw.

Preferably, this will be someone the bird will know and be comfortable with so that the transition is less painful.

Parrots are intelligent, and macaws in particular form deep life bonds. These birds genuinely grieve when they lose their humans, so it's important that they have other people they regard as friends. I will look at this in more detail in Chapter twelve.

Adopting a large and long–lived bird like a Scarlet Macaw is not something that should be done on a whim. It's imperative that you understand what this species requires BEFORE you visit a breeder.

Chapter 2: Origins and Characteristics

Chapter 3: Scarlet Macaws as Pets

If you have yet to made the decision to bring a Scarlet Macaw into your life, there are a number of factors you should take into consideration before doing so. Finding a reputable breeder and locating a healthy bird are important, but there are some necessary preparations to be made before bringing your new companion home.

Chapter 3: Scarlet Macaws as Pets

What to Know Before You Buy

There's more to know before you buy a Scarlet Macaw than cost and what kind of equipment you will need to house and care for your bird. Consider each of the following factors carefully.

In Chapter nine we cover Veterinary Care and finding a suitable veterinarian. I would strongly recommend that you locate a veterinarian in your local area who is experienced with parrots before you buy your Scarlet Macaw to ensure that you have someone who can advise you on your macaw's health from the start. If you leave finding a veterinarian until you have purchased your companion bird, you carry the risk of not finding a suitably qualified person in your local area.

Human Health Considerations

In this book we cover some of the common health issues experienced by Scarlet Macaws and some of the zoonotic diseases i.e. a disease that can be transmitted from an animal to a human being. We have also touched on the issue of allergies that can be caused by companion birds such as people being allergic to the dander. Before making the decision to bring a companion bird into your life, we strongly recommend that you take advice from your doctor and veterinarian so that you have a full understanding of any risks and implications to your own health.

Chapter 3: Scarlet Macaws as Pets

Macaws Live a Long Time

A well-cared for Scarlet Macaw can easily live to 75 years of age.

The very first question you have to ask yourself is whether or not you are willing to potentially devote decades of your own life to properly care for this bird no matter what changes in your life and that of your family.

Depending at what point in your life you adopt a macaw, he may well outlive you. What's more, no one can predict the future. If something happens to you, what will happen to your bird? Are you willing to make the necessary preparations for his continued care once you are no longer here? We will discuss how to plan for your bird's care after your death later in the book.

Every decision you make about your lifestyle and living circumstances from the moment you bring your Scarlet Macaw home, must include a consideration of the bird's welfare as well as your own.

Macaws Have Emotional Needs

Scarlet Macaws need interaction with their humans. These are highly social creatures. In the wild, they mate for life.

This is a bird that craves companionship, and in the absence of a "significant other," will bond deeply with you.

If you are not prepared to meet your macaw's physical and

psychological needs, please rethink your choice of pet before you commit to a Scarlet Macaw.

You are not only taking on an intelligent creature with real emotional needs, you are thinking of adopting a pet who could well outlive you.

On-going Socialization

No matter how bonded you may become with your Scarlet Macaw, the bird will still need to be handled daily and given adequate intellectual stimulation to keep it friendly and socialized.

Macaws that are feeling neglected or that are just plain bored, will act out. You need to plan on hand feeding your pet as much as possible, giving the bird physical affection, and providing lots of toys.

When you see just how destructive a bored macaw can be, you won't begrudge a single cent spent on toys!

Time outside the Cage

Parrot ownership is not to be taken lightly. Also, macaws require lots of time outside of their cages. They're simply too large and active to be confined to their enclosure for extended periods of time. Scarlet Macaws must have an engaged family who enjoy spending time with them and be given plenty of time to fly around. They cannot be relegated to a cage all day and ignored.

This not only means you will have to deal with "accidents" outside the cage, but also with your macaw's natural curiosity. It's highly possible you will have to devote an entire room in your home just for your bird.

You should allow your Scarlet Macaw to have at least two hours a day outside its cage but the more the better.

Aggressive Chewing

Scarlet Macaws like to chew — aggressively — and they are equipped with strong beaks that can cause absolute devastation. Remember, these birds are highly skilled rainforest foragers.

Provide your bird with a lot of wooden chew toys, perches, play areas and other means of stimulation. Chewing also helps to keep the bird's beak worn down, which is an essential component of its on–going healthcare.

Loud Squawking

If you live in a situation where noise can be a problem, think about ways to sound proof your bird room. Apartment dwellers need to ponder their choice of the Scarlet Macaw very carefully. The neighbors may not appreciate living next to a unit with a bird that is capable of raising the roof with its raucous calls.

Chapter 3: Scarlet Macaws as Pets

Other Pets and Children

Mixing a Scarlet Macaw with other pets is largely dependent on the personalities of the animals involved. Macaws are large enough that the altercation could end up being very unpleasant for any party in the mix.

Macaws do not tend to be aggressive by nature, but any animal, if cornered, will attempt to defend itself. Certainly you should never leave animals of different species unsupervised.

As for housing macaws with other birds, given the size of the Scarlet Macaw, this is really only advisable in an outdoor aviary setting.

A Scarlet Macaw is not appropriate as a child's pet. The birds are a challenge for a novice bird–owning adult. This is

Chapter 3: Scarlet Macaws as Pets

not to say that a child cannot be involved in the care of a macaw, but only with adult supervision and instruction.

Animals react to the manner in which they are treated. A Scarlet Macaw is capable of delivering a considerable bite if frightened or angered. In such an exchange with an animal, in all fairness, you have to evaluate who is really at fault, the bird or the child.

If a child had not been taught to act kindly and respectfully towards any animal, the creature can hardly be blamed for its instinctual reaction.

Remember, however, that macaws live a long time. If you bring one into the household when your children are small, they'll grow up thinking of the bird as a member of the family.

Over time, as your children get to know the bird and understand what it needs, their level of responsibility and independent interaction with the bird can and should grow.

Daily Maintenance

You will have daily maintenance chores for your Scarlet Macaw, including cleaning and disinfecting the bird's cage. Food and water must also be changed daily.

These chores will be interspersed with more extensive cleaning routines, weekly and monthly. Do not make the mistake of thinking there's anything "low maintenance" about a Scarlet Macaw.

Chapter 3: Scarlet Macaws as Pets

What about Wing Clipping?

Sometimes first-time parrot owners are advised to have their pet's wings clipped. For advocates of this frankly barbaric procedure, the argument is that a bird with clipped wings is safer. Nothing could be farther from the truth.

In mutilating a bird's wings, you rob the creature of its greatest natural ability – flight. This is a bird's natural first defense mechanism so that if faced with danger, they can fly away. Certainly young birds, or those who are frightened for any reason, can fly around in a panic and potentially harm themselves by crashing into things.

Wing clipping, however, is cruel and completely unnecessary. The only benefit in such an extreme "solution" is to a timid bird owner. Learning to gently and appropriately handle your Scarlet Macaw is part of the responsibility you are assuming.

Young birds that have been subjected to wing clipping are crippled for life. Their chest muscles will never develop appropriately, so even if their feathers are allowed to grow back, they will never become skilled flyers.

Many macaws begin to pluck their own feathers after their wings are clipped, likely as a sign of frustration that they cannot follow their natural instincts. This dissatisfaction can also play out with episodes of aggression and other negative behaviors.

Chapter 3: Scarlet Macaws as Pets

Beyond these very real ethical concerns, wing clipping that is handled incorrectly can harm the bird severely. The bleeding that results can be extensive enough to lead to death. The long-term negative consequences of wing clipping far outweigh any erroneously perceived benefit.

As a bond of trust grows between you and your Scarlet Macaw, handling your pet will be simple and natural. Your bird will learn to respond to your voice, and even to "commands". This bonding process does not develop overnight, however, and patience is required on your part.

Be assured that you and your bird will learn together — and since you will be together for a long time, the "good" times will far outweigh the initial period of getting to know each other.

Scarlet Macaws are highly intelligent. Your bird will take its cues from you. You never want to yell at a bird, or approach it suddenly. Stay calm, regardless of the situation, and show your bird that you are its "safe place". Remember, you will be the primary relationship in your macaw's life.

Tips for Buying a Scarlet Macaw

The last thing you want to do is invest a considerable amount of money in an unhealthy bird. As a result, you must do the legwork to find a reputable breeder or rescuer. The best way to find a reputable breeder is to consult a legitimate organization, such as the North American Parrot Society or the Parrot Society of the UK, to ask your avian veterinarian, or to ask other parrot owners for recommendations.

You can also check Petfinder (www.petfinder.org) for rescue organizations that have Scarlet Macaws for adoption. Check out the resources in this chapter and in the back of the book for links that will help you find a Scarlet Macaw for purchase or for adoption.

Never blindly purchase a parrot. Be sure to visit the breeder (or the rescue organization) first. If the breeder runs an open aviary, ask him to take you on a tour of the aviary. Is the facility clean? Are the cages clean? Do the birds look healthy? You want to find a facility that is well maintained, obviously clean, with proper ventilation and good lighting.

As you approach the birds being offered for sale, make sure that they are not stressed and that they do not overreact to your presence.

Unclean, unkempt living conditions and birds that look unhealthy or scared are all warnings signs that you should look for another breeder. If you have any doubts at all, it is best to keep looking.

In addition, do some background research before making your final decision. Google the breeders name online to determine what, if anything, bird owners are saying.

A healthy bird will generally:

- Have been weaned at an appropriate age
- Have bright eyes
- Be energetic and active
- Have a healthy appetite

The best breeders will not allow a bird to go to his new home until he has been fully weaned. Some breeders will sell babies shortly after they are born and will allow their new family to visit until the bird becomes fully weaned, often between three and a half and four months of age. Opt for a breeder who places an emphasis on socializing the baby. A well-socialized, imprinted bird (a bird that has connected with a human from an early age) will have a much easier time bonding with his or her new family members.

Chapter 3: Scarlet Macaws as Pets

Buying a Scarlet Macaw from an aviary helps to ensure that you find a healthy, well-socialized companion bird. That is not to say, however, that all aviaries operate according to the highest and most desirable standards.

More than One?

If you are a first-time parrot owner, it is not a good idea to buy a pair of Scarlet Macaws. Although it is true that this species mates for life, it's a mistake to think that having two will in any way negate your need to be an active presence in the emotional life of the birds.

You'll just have two affectionate, needy animals demanding your attention. And don't lose sight of the fact — ever — that Scarlet Macaws are one of the largest of parrots. With two birds you will need twice the room with twice the commitment and dedication.

Male or Female?

There really is no difference in temperament between the genders with Scarlet Macaws. Both make excellent pets.

It is much more important to concentrate on the factors of good health and socialization in choosing a macaw than worrying about picking a male or a female. They both look similar, although the tail feathers of males may be longer than females while the beaks of males may be slightly larger.

Judge the Bird's Demeanor

Scarlet Macaws are, by nature, curious and intelligent. The macaw should appear engaged, and should not be sitting off by itself. If a bird is sitting alone with feathers fluffed and the area is not chilly, the macaw is likely ill.

Ask the breeder to handle the bird and to allow you to see it more closely. Look for any sign of discharge from the eyes or nose, and make sure the area under and around the tail (the vent) is clean.

Handle the Macaw

With the breeder's permission and without distressing the bird, try to feel the chest (keel), which should be muscular and firm. If you can feel the bone, the parrot is too thin.

The Scarlet Macaw's general attitude should be happy. The bird should look healthy, and should exhibit a calm demeanor that will indicate it has been properly socialized.

Request a Vet Exam

Ask to have the macaw examined by a qualified avian veterinarian. If the breeder objects, you may want to reconsider. Provided adequate health records can be produced and verified, a new examination may not be essential, but you do want proof of good health.

Chapter 3: Scarlet Macaws as Pets

Good breeders should be not only willing, but proud to display the quality of the birds in their care.

Expect to Answer Questions

Breeders become quite attached to their birds, and are more than aware of the serious commitment involved in adopting a long-lived creature like a Scarlet Macaw. The breeder will want to know that the bird is going to a good home where it will receive proper care. Don't be surprised if the owner of the aviary has as many questions for you as you do for him.

Neither side should be put off by the questions and answers in this negotiatory process. It is quite proper for there to be more involved in the adoption of a Scarlet Macaw than cash on the table.

The Bird's Welfare Comes First

The bottom line for you and for the breeder should always be the welfare of the bird. That is the primary concern, and in the best of all possible worlds, you will maintain a relationship with the breeder in the future.

Especially if you are a first-time parrot owner, it is invaluable to have someone to whom you can turn for expert advice. The better your relationship with the breeder, the better for all concerned.

Costs and Other Considerations

Although prices will vary by breeder, you can expect to pay approximately $1,200 / £780 per bird. Often you will see pairs of macaws offered at a "discount" of $1,800 to $2,000 / £1,170 to £1,300.

This, of course, raises the question of owning more than one Scarlet Macaw but however tempting, please be realistic as to what you can manage for your sake and your pets.

Projected Costs

Please note that all costs are estimates at the time of writing and that currency rates of exchange are subject to daily variations.

Scarlet Macaw bird
Prices vary by breeder but average:
$1,200 / £780

Pairs are often offered at a discount:
$1,800 to $2,000 / £1,170 to £1,300

Chapter 3: Scarlet Macaws as Pets

Chapter 3: Scarlet Macaws as Pets

Stainless steel cage
$1,200 to $2,500 / £780 to £1,625

External playground (if not included with cage)
$100 to $200 / £65 to £130

Travel carrier
$100 to $150 / £65 to £97.50

Pellet food (ongoing expense)
(per 25 pounds / 11.34 kgs), approx. $45 / £29.25

Diet which is augmented by fresh vegetables and fruits means prices will vary locally. Can be supplemented with freeze-dried fruit and vegetable treats purchased in bulk from 1 to 5 lbs (0.45 kgs to 2.27 kgs) in a price range of $6 to $25 (£3.90 to £16.25).

Mineral block
$8 to $10 / £5.20 to £6.50

16 ounce / 0.5 liter water bottle
$35 to $40 / £22.75 to £26

Stainless steel food bowls 20 ounces / 0.57 kgs
$15 to $20 / £9.75 to £13

Bird harnesses
$30 to $50 / £19.50 to £32.50

Chew toys (ongoing expense)
$25 to $60 / £16.25 to £39 per toy

Estimated Set–Up Costs (Single Macaw):

$2,764 to $4,300 / £1,796.60 to £2,795

Ongoing Overheads

Start-up costs are, well, just the start. You also have to consider the ongoing cost of care. Some of the ongoing costs include:

An annual vet exam. This may include blood work and vaccinations.

Food. If you have a green thumb, you can cut down on the costs of fruits and vegetables by growing your own. Ensure that you do not use any chemicals or pesticides as these could affect the health of your bird.

Toys. Macaws have strong beaks. Toys will not last forever, so you will need to resupply as needed.

Grooming. You will have to pay to have your bird's nails clipped, unless you already have experience clipping a parrot's nail or you are willing to learn from a professional.

In addition, you should always be prepared for the - what ifs! What if your macaw gets sick? What if he develops a serious, long-term illness? What if he is somehow injured?

Chapter 3: Scarlet Macaws as Pets

Can you realistically afford to pay for emergency medical expenses?

If you do not have money on hand for an emergency, are you financially able to set money aside each week, each month, or regularly to build-up savings you can use in case of an emergency? Additionally, you may also be able to use pet insurance to help defray veterinary costs.

Seriously think about the answers to those questions. If you cannot realistically afford to care for a parrot now, consider waiting until you have the necessary finances to bring one home.

Aviaries

The following pages provide just a partial list of the aviaries available in the United States and the United Kingdom. It is not intended as a comprehensive source, nor does the author specifically endorse any of these facilities. I recommend that you spend some time researching aviaries in your area. It may be helpful to contact your local avian veterinarian for a recommendation.

You can spend some further time checking forums online to see what feedback is available but nothing beats personal recommendations.

Chapter 3: Scarlet Macaws as Pets

Aviaries and Breeders in the U.S.A.

Alabama
Tweety Bird Aviary
Huntsville, AL
http://www.tweetybirdaviary.com

Irena's Aviary
Blountsville, AL 35031
205 429 4367

Arkansas
Fancy Feathers Aviary and Supplies
Little Rock, AR
501-453-4574

California
EMR Exotic Bird Breeder
San Diego, CA
www.emrexoticbirdbreeder.com

Melzano's Parrot Place
San Diego, CA
www.melzanosparrotplace.com

Feathered Nest
Northern CA, CA 95688
925-698-0191

Ara Aviaries California
28115 Dorothy dr.
Agoura Hills Los Angeles, CA 91301
805-338-3549

Cedar Hill Birds
Lodi, CA 95240
http://www.cedarhillbirds.com

Ozark Exotics
Huntington Beach, CA
714-248-6827

Colorado
Avalon Aviary
Loveland, CO
www.avalonaviary.com

Connecticut
Diane's Parrot Place
RT. 6 and RT. 61
Woodbury, CT 06798
http://dianesparrotplace.weebly.com

Florida
Best Bird Aviary
Summerfield, FL
www.thebestbird.com

Lone Palm Aviary
West Palm Beach, FL
www.lpbirds.com

Birds 4 You
Trinity, FL
www.birds4you.org

Featherheads
Lithia, FL 33547
(813) 679-4961

Feather's Bird Shoppe, Inc.
Reddick, FL 32686
352-369-0677

Georgia
East Coast Birds
Saint Marys, GA 31558,
912-674-4841

Iowa
Tree Top Aviary and Rescue
1403 Washington Ave
Cedar Rapids, IA 52403
http://www.treetopsrescue.org/

Zimmerman Pets
Sioux City, IA 51108
http://www.zimmermanpets.com

Chapter 3: Scarlet Macaws as Pets

Louisiana
AJ's Aviary
Youngsville, LA 70592
http://ajsaviary.net/

Agape Aviary
Lafayette
http://agapeaviary.com/

Missouri
Blue Angel Aviaries
14244 Dry Fork Rd.
Festus, MO 63028
636–931–2784

Gateway Aviaries
St. Louis, MO 63119
314-374-1876

North Carolina
Bella's Aviary
Kiril Poibrenski
Charlotte, North Carolina
www.bellaaviary.com

Lone Eagle Aviaries
Leasburg, NC 27291
703 606-1884

Nebraska
Love-A-Lop- Farm
Allen, NE 68710
www.lovealop.com

New Hampshire
CoooCooo's Nest
Derry, NH
www.cooocooosnest.com

Parrot Safari
Londonderry, NH 03053
www.parrotsafari.com

New Jersey
World of Birds
Chester, NJ
www.worldofbirds.net

Birds by Joe LLC
Middlesex, NJ
www.birdsbyjoe.com

New York
Maria's Birds
North Tonawanda, NY
www.mariasbirds.com

For Birds Only
Mineola, NY 11501
www.forbirdsonlyny.com

Ohio
In a Pickle Parrots
Broadview Heights, OH
www.inapickleparrots.com

BirdWalk
549 Liberty St
Painesville, OH 44077
www.birdwalkstore.com

Oklahoma
Sooner Parrot Place
Oklahoma City, OK 73135
www.soonerparrotplace.com

Oregon
The Parrot Patch
Eugene, OR 97404
541-463-9564

Pennsylvania
Birds by Stephanie
Aliquippa, PA 15001
(724) 417-8146

Jr's Feathered Friends
Kunkletown, PA 18058
610-895-4092

Tennessee
The Bird Hut, Dickson, TN
www.the-bird-hut.com

Adventure Birds of Bom Aqua
9600 Highway 46
Bon Aqua, TN 37025
931-670-3204

Texas
Bayoubirdnest.Com
Beaumont, TX 77713
409-347-8221

Jadies Birdnest
Katy, TX 77493, 832-404-4444

To Parrots With Love
Houston, TX 77064
713-504-3525

Virginia
Birdie Brains Aviary
2267 Lancashire Dr.
North Chesterfield, VA 23235
www.birdiebrainsaviary.com

KB's Exotic Birds
Suffolk, VA 23434
757-539-8883

Wisconsin
Roxanne's Birds
Milwaukee, WI 53208-2246
www.roxannesbirds.webs.com

Aviaries and Breeders in the U.K.

Barrett Watson Parrots
www.barrettwatsonparrots.co.uk

Bird Trader
www.birdtrader.co.uk

Birds4Sale
www.birds4sale.co.uk

Birdtrek
www.birdtrek.co.uk

Parrot–Link
www.parrot-link.co.uk/

Preloved
www.preloved.co.uk

Premium Parrots
www.premiumparrots.com

Birds for Sale in the UK
http://birdsforsaleinuk.blogspot.com

Chapter 3: Scarlet Macaws as Pets

Pros and Cons of Owning a Scarlet Macaw

As with any companion animal, what one person considers to be a "plus" or a "pro" of owning a Scarlet Macaw may be another person's "minus" or "con". With that in mind, remember these key points:

- These birds have genuine emotional needs. Your Scarlet Macaw will regard you as its mate, and love you accordingly. That bond is deep and real for these affectionate and intelligent birds. This is a wonderful aspect of life with a macaw, but it is a chosen "relationship" and a huge commitment on your part.

- To keep a macaw's level of socialization intact, they need physical human interaction every day as well as free flight time. This is decidedly a plus for most people. Scarlet Macaws love to be handled! But again, if you're a very busy person, you could see this need as a burden.

- Destructive chewing with just about any species is a definite negative that has to be managed. The macaw is just being who and what it is, not an intentionally "bad" pet. Making sure your bird has enough chew toys is up to you. That being said, watching a macaw use its beak is fascinating. They can accomplish things with their beak we can't pull off with both hands!

- Macaws are not soft spoken! Again, this is a plus or minus depending on your circumstances. Squawking

Chapter 3: Scarlet Macaws as Pets

is not something neighbors in an apartment complex will appreciate, but if you enjoy talking to your bird — in his language or yours — you should always know exactly what your pet is thinking!

Apart from these considerations, Scarlet Macaws are big, beautiful parrots that require spacious cages or outdoor aviaries.

They also have long life spans. This means you can have a devoted, loving companion for decades, which is what any of us crave in our animal friends.

It's an added responsibility, since your bird may well outlive you, but for most people, a parrot's longevity is part of their tremendous appeal.

Chapter 4: Bird Proofing Your Home

Your Scarlet Macaw must have time out of his cage each day to stretch his wings and just hang out with the family. However, before you even bring your macaw home, you should be prepared to bird proof the areas of your home in which your bird will be allowed.

Chapter 4: Bird Proofing Your Home

Scarlet Macaws are known for gnawing on wood with their beaks in the wild and they will do the same in your home. Your wood cabinet? It is the perfect chew toy, especially if he is bored, unless you take the proper measures to bird proof.

Keep the following in mind as you decide what in your home needs bird proofing:

Birds love wires. One bite through a wire – to a lamp, a telephone, a television, a computer, or another appliance – could very well spell disaster for your macaw. An electric shock could seriously injure or kill your bird. As a result, you must hide or protect all wires from your bird. Some owners recommend putting the wires high off of the ground and out of reach. Remember, however, that Scarlet Macaws are tree toppers and like to go on high places.

You can purchase plastic tubing at home improvement stores and wire covers at other retail stores to protect the wires. The tubing is generally thick and round and protects the wires from your bird's strong bite. However, always keep an eye on what your bird is up to.

Cover furniture. Your parrot may inadvertently defecate on your favorite chair or on the couch, so make sure to protect your furniture by placing an old towel or blanket on it while he sits or plays on the furniture.

Use plastic siding. Macaws naturally chew on wood, so be sure to protect any wooden cabinets or other furniture in your home before allowing your bird out of the cage. Some owners use plastic siding or a sheet of plastic to cover the sides of wooden furniture, such as shelves, entertainment centers and cabinets.

Turn off all ceiling fans. A flying bird can hit a moving ceiling fan, resulting in serious injury or even death. Make it a habit of always turning off the ceiling fans. Some experts recommend completely disabling your ceiling fan or replacing it altogether so there is absolutely no chance of forgetting to turn it off when your parrot is out of his cage.

Keep the toilet seat down. Make it a habit to keep the toilet seat down in all of the bathrooms in your home. Birds have wandered into bathrooms and have drowned in the toilet, so get used to putting the toilet seat down, if you do not already do so.

Keep the bathroom door shut. If you fear you may forget to put the toilet seat down, start keeping the bathroom door shut so there is no possibility of your macaw getting in the bathroom. You could also make it a habit to do both – put the toilet seat down and shut the door – just as a precaution in case you or someone else in the family forgets to do one or the other. That way, hopefully you have at least one layer of protection.

Put lids on pots of boiling water and other food. Some experts recommend never allowing your parrot in the kitchen while you are cooking or to keep him confined in his cage while you are cooking. If your bird is out in another room, he may very well wander into the kitchen, making it essential to keep lids on any boiling water or food

Chapter 4: Bird Proofing Your Home

that is cooking. Personally, I would never risk leaving my parrot out while cooking.

Shut windows. Shut all the windows in a room when your parrot is going to be out. If you have screens in the windows, you can leave them open if you remain vigilant and make sure your macaw does not start nibbling on the screen.

Use window coverings. You have probably, at one point in your life, seen or have heard about a bird that flew straight into a shut window. That bird either became dazed or endured a fatal blow. Window coverings – such as blinds or curtains – will alert your bird that the window is there and will help him avoid the serious consequences that can result from flying into a closed window.

Be careful of mirrors. Mirrors pose the same problem as closed windows. Your parrot may very well just fly right into it, albeit accidentally. Train your bird not to go near windows or cover them with a sheet or window coverings when not in use.

Take care when opening doors. Scarlet Macaws can and will fly out of an open door and they generally do not have the ability to find their way home again. As a result, if your macaw spends time near a door into and out of your home, you must take precautions. If you have two doors, make sure only one door is open at a time. A door left wide open is an invitation for a curious bird to go exploring. If you have one door leading into the home and need to bring groceries into the house, for example, put your macaw into

Chapter 4: Bird Proofing Your Home

his cage until you have brought everything in and can shut the door.

If you do not have two doors, you are going to have to become more creative to find a way to keep your bird away from the door. Putting a sheet in front of the door, so you have to go behind it to get in and out is one way to protect your bird. As this is no guarantee, it is always best to close all doors and windows.

Beware of toxins. Now that you have a Scarlet Macaw in your home, you have to think of things that you might not have thought about before. The following are all toxins which you should be aware of:

- Scented candles, potpourris, air fresheners, plug-ins and incense are toxic to all birds. A lot of people enjoy burning scented candles or using air fresheners, plug-ins or incense to give their home a fresh scent. Never use these with a parrot in your home as they can be toxic.

- Using hairspray, perfume and deodorant in aerosol cans in the same space as your macaw can both be toxic to your bird and can cause him respiratory distress, which could lead to serious illness and even death.

- New carpet. If you are having new carpet installed in your home, consider having your macaw spend time with another family member at their home. New

Chapter 4: Bird Proofing Your Home

carpet emits formaldehyde fumes, which can be deadly to birds.

- Paint and varnish are also both potentially fatal to birds, so be sure your parrot is not in the home when you paint or use varnish.

- Smoke from cigars, pipes, and cigarettes also threatens to cause respiratory problems in birds. Avoid smoking or else you risk your bird becoming seriously ill.

- Cleaning products pose a risk to all birds, so do not spray or use them when your bird is in the same space. There are some great non-toxic options now obtainable, many of which should be available at your local store.

- Non-stick cookware, which leaks toxic fumes regardless of whether the food is cooked properly or is burned, is extremely toxic to all birds. If your macaw is in the same room while you are using the non-stick cookware, he could die within minutes. Replace, if possible, all non-stick cookware with stainless steel and never allow your bird to be in the kitchen while you are cooking.

Making a safe home for your Scarlet Macaw is very much like baby proofing a home. It is essential to ensuring your bird's well-being. In addition to bird proofing your home, you can do several things to keep your bird happy and

Chapter 4: Bird Proofing Your Home

occupied and his mind off of chewing something he should not chew.

A final note about bird proofing: Make sure you bird proof before you bring your Scarlet Macaw home. Ultimately, it is for his safety and well-being. As you and he become accustomed to living together, you may discover other ways to make your home safer and techniques that may have been mentioned here that just do not work for you.

The key is to make a conscious effort to bird proof your home and to, as best as you can, always keep an eye on your macaw when he is not confined to his cage. Remember though, that bird proofing does not mean you can leave your macaw to roam freely.

Chapter 5: Home Sweet Home

To be really prepared to bring your Scarlet Macaw home and to experience a positive transition and bonding experience, ensure you complete your shopping for equipment first and the bird itself second.

The following items represent the major initial purchases. As you get to know and understand your new pet, you'll be able to buy the things your bird really likes. That familiarity will cut down on trial and error acquisitions in the years to come.

Chapter 5: Home Sweet Home

The first and greatest expense is your Scarlet Macaw's cage. This is NOT an area where you want to scrimp on costs.

Picking the Perfect Cage

The recommended minimum cage size for your Scarlet Macaw is 2.5' wide x 4' deep x 5' tall / 0.76m x 1.22m x 1.52m.

Remember, however, you are adopting one of the largest of all the parrots. Get the biggest cage you can afford. Make sure that the bars of the cage are spaced at a distance no greater than 1 inch / 2.54 cm.

Bars that are more widely spaced raise the potential of the bird getting its head, or feet caught between the bars. Serious injury or even death can result.

Important Cage Features

The bird's habitat should contain a variety of well-placed perches. It's important to encourage your Scarlet Macaw to exercise its feet since arthritis is an issue with this species as they age.

The bottom of the cage should be outfitted with a metal grate to allow excrement to fall into the tray below. Line that tray with paper or some form of material to facilitate cage cleaning.

Chapter 5: Home Sweet Home

Be extremely careful never to place food trays or water sources within the cage under perches where they can become fouled by the bird's droppings.

Be Cautious About Materials

In selecting items for you macaw's habitat, be especially careful that all components are free of both zinc and lead. Plastics should be BPA and PVC free. This precaution also extends to any painted portions of the habitat.

Scarlet Macaws chew constantly, so make sure whatever they're chewing on is completely safe. Even if the bird is just "checking something out" it could accidentally be exposed to a harmful chemical.

Chapter 5: Home Sweet Home

Cage Costs

A stainless steel cage with self-locking entrances that falls within these dimensions will cost between $1,200 to $2,500 / £780 to £1,625.

Cage Placement

Do not place your macaw's cage in front of a window, or subject your pet to a draft. Normal room temperatures are fine for Scarlet Macaws, but they do not tolerate temperatures of 80 F / 26.7 C or higher.

Also, don't strand the poor bird in a back bedroom! Scarlet Macaws are social animals. They want to see and be a part of what's going on.

Pick a well-travelled area in the house. Put the cage up against a wall as this will give your bird a greater sense of security and ensure it gets plenty of natural sunlight during the day. Natural sunlight is essential for the development of vitamin K which contributes to healthy skin and feathers.

Finally, don't put the cage close to the kitchen. Never use any cooking appliance or implement with a non-stick coating in the same room – or preferably in the same house — with any companion bird. They emit fumes that can kill your Scarlet Macaw. My recommendation is to replace all non-stick cookware with stainless steel.

Chapter 5: Home Sweet Home

Cage Maintenance

Since you will need access to your macaw's habitat on a daily basis, remember to consider your own needs in picking a location for the cage.

A clean cage or aviary will help ensure your parrot's good health. Be sure to clean your bird's cage often, keeping the following in mind:

- Change paper on the bottom of the cage daily. The bottom of the cage will catch your bird's droppings, and you do not want to leave them sitting there for too long. If you purchased a cage with a bottom that is easy to remove, changing the paper should take only a few minutes each day and can be part of your daily routine.

- Clean the inside of the cage regularly. Remove the bottom and vacuum any excess seed and dispose of the paper. Wash the bottom of the cage with soap and water then rinse and dry. Wipe down the bars of the cage. Do a thorough cleaning of your bird's entire cage at least once a month or more often if necessary, ensuring you remove your bird during the process. I would recommend natural disinfectants like vinegar for washing and baking soda for scrubbing. Ensure that it is thoroughly washed with water and left to dry. Never use any household chemicals that could be toxic for your pet.

- Remove all of the bowls and wash them with soap and water. Rinse the bowls thoroughly to ensure you remove any residue from the soap. Let the bowls air dry or dry them thoroughly with a clean towel before refilling with water and food and placing them back into the cage. Be sure to wash food and water bowls regularly. Failure to do so can lead to a build-up in bacteria, which could result in illness in your bird.

- Clean the perches. Wipe off any droppings from the perch then wash with soap and water. Rinse thoroughly to remove any soap residue and let air dry, preferably in the sunshine, if possible. If not, just allow to dry out on a countertop.

- Thoroughly wash all toys, including mirrors, and ropes in the cage. Read cleaning instructions as some allow for washing in the dishwasher while others can be washed in the washing machine. If there are no specific washing instructions, wash with mild soap and water then rinse thoroughly. Set in the sun to allow to air dry. In colder months, air drying may not be possible so you can dry with a clean, dry towel or allow to air dry inside on a countertop.

- Make sure you keep your bird's cage clean to avoid illness or a build-up of waste. If you give your bird fruit and vegetables and he throws them on the bottom of the cage, throw them away when he is done eating to keep the food from rotting, which can attract bugs and cause problems.

An Outdoor Option?

All companion birds will benefit from having a large outdoor enclosure to allow for greater freedom of movement. The critical considerations, however, are the bird's safety both from the elements and from potential predators.

Beyond that, the only limitations on outdoor aviaries are space, budget and your creativity. Any outdoor structure needs to follow the same cautions in regard to bar spacing and materials used as those that apply to indoor enclosures. It's also important to incorporate a double entrance.

Use a Double Door Design

You want to be certain that you can enter the enclosure with your macaw in a secure travel crate, close one door behind you, and then go into the main aviary through a second door. Both should be closed before the bird is released.

This double–door system is a crucial safeguard against accidental releases. Even if your bird is not prone to trying to fly away, all it takes is one moment of fear, and you could be watching helplessly as your beloved pet takes off.

Chapter 5: Home Sweet Home

Plans and Ideas Online

To get ideas for aviary designs, simply run an online search. Do–it–yourself bird owners have created some fantastic spaces for their pets. If you can't complete the construction yourself, work with a contractor. Most will give estimates for a nominal fee.

If you have the space and the money to provide this extra room for your Scarlet Macaw, your bird will be much happier and healthier in the long run.

Additionally, with the added intellectual stimulation, your bird will be much less likely to become bored and destructive inside your home.

Chapter 5: Home Sweet Home

Macaws Love Playgrounds

When you shop for a cage, you'll see that many of them have an outside playground mounted on top. This area may include a branch, big perch or even a swing that the bird can use during free flight time and include toys for him to play with and to chew. It should have its own tray to collect droppings.

If the cage you're considering doesn't come with a unit of this type, you can buy one and attach it, which is highly recommended.

Often Scarlet Macaws will return to the top of their cage to signal they're ready to go back inside, or you can develop a routine of calling your bird to its perch when play time is over.

Think of the cage–top playground as a useful "home base". When your macaw is really accustomed to being in your home, it may well sit on its external perch and watch what you're doing without flying around the room much if at all.

Stand–alone playgrounds sell for $100 to $200 / £65 to £130.

Instead of purchasing a play area, some people prefer making their own activity center. A sturdy table top, branches, and toys creatively placed can make the perfect play areas.

Place play areas throughout your home, in the areas in which your bird is allowed, to keep his attention off of destroying furniture, cabinets and other belongings. Even

Chapter 5: Home Sweet Home

though you may provide your Scarlet Macaw with an abundance of toys, you still must bird proof your home for his safety.

Place perches throughout your home, again in the areas in which your macaw is allowed access, so your bird can hang out with you and avoid ruining furniture. If you spend evenings lounging on the couch and watching television, consider placing perches next to the couch so your parrot can hang out next to you.

Toys, Toys and More Toys

Provide your macaw with plenty of toys – chew toys, rope toys, etc. ensuring they are non-toxic, BPA and PVC free – and make sure he has toys in all areas of the home to which he has access. The more toys your bird has, the more likely he is going to be mentally and physically stimulated and the less likely he is going to become destructive.

Chapter 5: Home Sweet Home

Chapter 6: Daily Care

Macaws like both variety and quality in their diet, and can easily become bored with their "menu". After all, you don't like to eat the same thing every day, do you?

Your macaw's diet will be made up of pellets, seeds, fresh fruit and vegetables. It is worth shopping around and be guided by the breeder who supplied you your macaw.

Chapter 6: Daily Care

Diet and Nutrition

Your bird's diet should, however, be based primarily on specialized pellet food to ensure proper nutrition. Pellets will make up 60% to 70% of your macaw's overall food intake. This makes life much easier for you, and it allows you to monitor how much your bird eats daily. Detecting changes in appetite are an important part of ongoing preventive healthcare.

Make pellet food available for your bird at all times. Don't worry about your Scarlet Macaw overeating. By nature, macaws are foragers. The bird will "nibble" throughout the day, mimicking its wild feeding behavior.

An example of a popular food for macaws is Lafeber's Macaw Pellets, which sells for approximately $45 / £29.25 per 25 pounds / 11.34 kgs.

Although "fortified" seeds can also be used, these natural products contain more fat than pellets. Use seeds sparingly, and serve mixed with the pellet ration.

In the wild Scarlet Macaws have access to a varied selection of exotic fruits and food which you are unlikely to be able to source locally. They do however love variety and in addition to the standard list on the next page really enjoy pine nuts, pecans, almonds and pumpkin seeds in their shells.

If you have any concerns in respect of what is suitable or

the quantities, please check with the breeder you bought your pet from who will only be delighted to help and will no doubt suggest local produce suppliers. Alternatively, check with your avian veterinarian.

Appropriate fresh fruits and vegetables include:

- apples
- pears
- berries
- grapes
- mango
- bananas
- figs
- cranberries
- melons
- carrots
- turnips
- yams
- broccoli
- cucumber
- celery
- sweet potatoes
- peppers
- dark green leafy vegetables such as kale

Chapter 6: Daily Care

Vegetables are more nutritious than fruits, which have a high natural sugar content and should be offered daily, with uneaten food removed from the cage within 24 hours.

In purchasing fruits and vegetables, it is wise to buy organic produce. There are serious problems with contamination in our food supply coming from insecticides as well as chemicals that leach into groundwater. Be sure to wash all produce before giving it to your pet.

Do NOT feed your Scarlet Macaw avocados or fruit seeds, or allow your pet to have access to caffeine, alcohol, or chocolate. Even with their unusually strong digestive systems, these substances can cause serious harm to your bird. It is best to check with your avian veterinarian before introducing any foods other than specialist pellets. Please note that the list on the previous page is not exhaustive.

Although it's perfectly acceptable and naturally healthy to give your macaw fresh fruits and vegetables, many bird owners opt for freeze-dried fruit and vegetable treats such as cranberries, apricots, peas, carrots and whole corn due to ease of storage. Most are purchased in bulk from 1 to 5 lbs (0.45 kgs to 2.27 kgs) in a price range of $6 to $25 (£3.90 to £16.25).

Treats

Nuts such as Brazil, walnuts, pecans and macadamias, all in their shell and unsalted along with seeds are always a winner but due to their high fat content it is best practice to

Chapter 6: Daily Care

give them as treats and rewards. The inclusion of infrequent carbohydrate snacks like graham crackers or unsalted whole-wheat crackers will also be welcomed. A supplemental treat would be some sprouted seeds which will provide a number of vitamins like A, B, C and E, and are considered a source of enzymes but it is very important that these are fresh, organic and properly cleaned and never left more than a day in their cage.

Food and Water Dispensers

For macaws, choose at least a 16 fluid ounce / 0.5 liter water bottle with a ball bearing "lixit" tip. Typically bottles of this size are made of glass, and the step and tip will be stainless steel. The average cost per bottle is $35 to $40 / £22.75 to £26.

Your bird should have a constant supply of clean, de-chlorinated water. Change the macaw's water supply daily to avoid any build-up of bacteria in the water bottle. Wash the bottle regularly and rinse thoroughly to remove any residue.

Stainless steel food bowls that can be attached to the side of the cage, which helps to prevent fouling from feces, are recommended. These should have a capacity of at least 20 ounces / 0.57 kgs and are priced at $15 to $20 / £9.75 to £13.

Mineral Block

Scarlet Macaws need a mineral block as a source of calcium and other nutrients that they would derive in their native habitat from visiting clay licks.

In the wild, the parrots eat clay to protect themselves from potentially toxic foods. In captivity, however, their diets are monitored, so no source of clay is required.

An example of such a product is the "Avian Specialties Manu Natural Essential Mineral Block for a Healthy Bird," which is appropriate for larger species. Expect to pay $8 to $10 / £5.20 to £6.50 per block.

Chew Toys

There really is no such thing as too many chew toys for a macaw. The more interesting items you give your pet, the less likely it will be to engage in destructive behaviors during free flight time.

Always pick the "extra-large" size of any item. Some of these toys, in order to be appropriate for a bird the size of a Scarlet Macaw, will be 20 inches / 50.8 cm or more in length and weigh as much as 4 lbs / 1.81 kgs.

You will see such items listed with descriptions like, "Destructible toy satisfies a bird's instinctual need to chew". Expect to pay $25 to $30 / £16.25 to £19.50 per toy and expect to replace the items often.

Chapter 6: Daily Care

As an example of a toy a Scarlet Macaw would like, Caitec Bird Supplies offers the Jumbo Boredom Buster Bird Toy. Although it is pricey at $60 / £39, this 12 lbs / 5.44 kgs hanging toy offers excellent variety.

It includes, "clunky, colorful wooden blocks tied with rope knots. Hung on a bird safe chain, this large bird toy provides wood, cotton rope and sisal rope textures that promote chewing, preening and exercise".

Although you don't want to overcrowd your bird's cage, make sure it has at least one or two toys of this type inside the enclosure, and more on the outside of the habitat. The goal is to keep the macaw interested while constructively directing its chewing.

Sleeping

When you turn out the lights, your bird should settle down for the night. If the bird has any trouble sleeping, take steps to ensure the room is sufficiently darkened. Your macaw will need a minimum of 10 hours of sleep each night. You have several options for ensuring your bird gets the sleep he needs.

Typically it is not necessary to cover a macaw's cage at night but if he is in a common living area, you can cover his cage with a blanket or a cage cover to dim the light so he can get the sleep he needs. Depending on his personality though he may not like this and make his feelings known loud and clear. However, if the area is noisy, he may not get adequate rest so keep in mind you might have to come up with an alternative plan.

One way to avoid worrying about your macaw getting proper sleep is to purchase a cage on wheels. That way, when it is time for him to sleep, you can wheel his cage into a quiet, darkened room.

Another option, which works for some families, is to purchase a separate cage specifically for your bird to sleep in. You can keep the cage in the area where he will sleep and put him there each night at bed time.

Chapter 6: Daily Care

Grooming and Bath Time

Although many novice bird keepers are surprised by this fact, your Scarlet Macaw will need to be bathed regularly in lukewarm, chlorine–free water to stay clean as overly dry skin and feather loss may mean a lack of macaw hygiene.

The general rule of thumb, according to experts, is to bathe your parrot between five and seven times during the warmer summer months and three to five times during the cold winter months. Your macaw will actually enjoy it!

The temperature for your bird's bath water really depends on what it prefers. Remember, however, your macaw should not be exposed to a temperature that is less than between 70 and 72 degrees Fahrenheit and 21.1 and 22.2 Celsius. Like people, birds have their own preferences, and you will get to know those preferences as you get to know your bird better.

You can bathe your macaw in one of several ways:

- Due to his size, the kitchen or bathroom sink may be the most suitable with the nozzle set to medium. Your macaw won't need any tutoring and will be well able to manage at their own pace, as long as they feel comfortable and have sufficient room. They will flap their wings and shake their tail feathers and enjoy themselves doing it.

- You can also give your macaw a "shower" by spraying or misting him with a water bottle.

Chapter 6: Daily Care

- If your bird has an outside aviary, put him in the aviary to get a shower in the rain. Remember, however, that the weather should be warm so he does not get sick.

You may want your Scarlet Macaw to join you in the shower. Install a perch in the shower, where your bird can stand, and bring him in the next time you take a shower. Give him plenty of room to flap his wings and do it at their pace. Remember; make sure the water is not too hot and not too cold.

Whilst you will not use soap or shampoo on your pet, you must take care to ensure that he does accidently come into contact with it while you are using them as they may prove toxic to him. If you have concerns about bathing your Scarlet Macaw or about water temperature, consult with your veterinarian.

Nail Clipping

The macaw's nails will also need to be trimmed, but if at all possible, have this procedure done by a professional to prevent injury to your pet. Some pet stores have professional grooming salons. You can also take your macaw to the vet and have the vet technician teach you how to properly cut your bird's nails.

If that is not possible, ask your breeder or a more experienced macaw owner to work with you through the first couple of clippings so you can learn how to handle the bird and how much to trim off the nails. If done incorrectly, it can cause serious injury.

Whenever you cut your bird's nails on your own, be sure to have a small bowl of flour nearby. Birds can get antsy, can jerk their foot, and in that movement, you may accidentally cut along the quick, resulting in bleeding. If you clip a nail too close to the quick and it begins to bleed, simply put his foot into flour and hold it there until the blood begins to congeal.

Some owners, to allow for less frequent nail trims, put a perch in their bird's cage that is designed to help keep the nails trimmed. Below is an example of such a perch:

www.funtimebirdy.com/pedicure-nail-trimming-macaw-bird-parrot-perch.html#.UcOA75zuyAY

Chapter 6: Daily Care

Tricks and Speech

One of the great pleasures of owning a Scarlet Macaw is the species' great capacity to learn both tricks and speech. The birds are adept at mimicking words and the sounds in your home.

So don't be startled if you suddenly hear your bird imitating your ringtones, or repeating lines from commercials. Really all that is involved in teaching a macaw to speak is exposing it to speech and associating key phrases with repetitive actions.

Predictable vocabulary will be assimilated first. Talk to your bird as if you expect it to start answering. Say hello and goodbye. Ask the macaw if it wants the carrot you're holding out. Be consistent with the words and phrases you use. The parrot will handle the rest. Macaws are very quick to catch on. They'll understand that the sounds they are making are getting a positive response and will start expanding what they're doing to get more of your attention.

When your macaw begins to mimic sounds or says the stray word, start naming things for the bird in a more purposeful way. Give it verbal cues that match activities. For instance, when the macaw accepts an offered treat, say, "Thank you!"

YouTube is an invaluable resource for parrot owners in regard to language lessons. Simply go to the site and search available videos for "teach parrot to talk".

Chapter 6: Daily Care

While not all of the videos you find will necessarily be specific to Scarlet Macaws, the methodology is identical, plus, it's helpful to see parrot owners interacting with their birds.

Conservative estimates place a Scarlet Macaw's ability to learn language at 10 to 15 words and/or phrases, but most parrot owners say their pets come closer to 20 to 25.

There's a great deal of debate about whether or not Scarlet Macaws actually understand what they're saying.

Certainly their capacity to understand human speech and respond appropriately is often to the point of being rather uncanny!

Tips for Teaching Tricks

You will soon discover that your Scarlet Macaw is quite capable of picking up all kinds of tricks, not just learning words and phrases.

The training process will go much faster if you build on what your pet does naturally. Watch the bird. If it has a habit of lifting one foot, work on turning that action into a cued "wave" or "handshake".

Use praise, treats and patience. Once your Scarlet Macaw realizes it's all a game, and that you're paying complete attention, the learning curve will start up fast. Don't be offended, however, if the bird thinks it's the instructor and you're the student.

Understanding Scarlet Macaw Behavior

Scarlet Macaws are highly affectionate birds, who, when properly socialized, welcome a hug or a cuddle. They can, however, get aggressive if they don't have enough stimulation, attention and entertainment.

Think of your bird like an incredibly brilliant toddler. His attention may be easily diverted from one thing to the next, but when you have his attention, he's completely engaged.

Your macaw will more or less think of you as a really funny looking bird, and treat you accordingly. This may extend to delivering little playful nips. This does not mean your bird is developing a biting habit, nor should you overreact or try to "discipline" your bird. He's not being "bad," he's just checking things out in a very bird-like fashion.

If your macaw is being aggressive, you'll know it! Then the best course of action is to just back away. Yelling at a macaw isn't going to do anything but get him to yell back. Allow your bird to calm down by being calm with him. Don't ever let a macaw know you're scared or intimidated, or you will have a bully on your hands.

With lots of engaging toys, interaction with you, and time out of the cage, biting should not be a problem. If your bird starts acting out, look to your own behavior first and figure out what you're not giving the macaw that it needs — starting with attention.

Handling Your Macaw

Although they are large, Scarlet Macaws are very cuddly and affectionate birds. Initially you'll both be getting used to each other. You may find it a little startling the first time your bird lands on your shoulder, but this is an excellent sign that your bonding is progressing nicely.

As with all birds, don't subject your macaw to loud noises or sudden movements. Speak softly and gently. Never shake the cage, or associate the bird's habitat in any way with "punishment".

Chapter 6: Daily Care

Create a stable routine for your macaw, and include your pet in the household. Macaws love interaction, and enjoy "conversations" with their humans.

When handling your macaw, hold the bird securely, but gently. Do not make the macaw feel as if it is being restrained. Many people mistake the phrase "control the bird" to imply force. Tailor your actions toward calming your macaw.

Never grab the bird or threaten it in any way. In most cases, you can simply invite the bird onto your shoulder or arm and it will happily "ride" along.

The first command you should teach your pet is "step up" or "perch". Offer your macaw your arm, and use the command while offering the bird a treat. Position the item in such a way that the macaw has to perch on your arm to get it.

Do this repeatedly until the bird will hop up on your arm with or without a proffered treat. This simple "trick" is the basis for being able to handle your bird reliably. You'll find yourself using it every day to return your macaw to its habitat, or to get him down off the curtain rods!

There are many variations on standard training routines. Again, YouTube is an invaluable resource. Parrot owners are understandably quite proud of their handsome friends, and share videos like the doting "parents" they are. As a new bird owner, you can learn a great deal from these videos, plus, new ones are being added every day.

It is important to understand that every macaw is an individual, with a unique personality and a different capacity to learn. Don't try to force your bird to do something just because you've watched another macaw do it online.

We can all watch child prodigies play the violin, but that doesn't mean we can pick up the instrument cold and do the same thing!

Using a Bird Harness

As an option for getting out and about with your macaw and ensuring that the bird is well exercised, consider looking into a bird flight harnesses.

While these units are not always a success with smaller species, they tend to work quite well with large birds like Scarlet Macaws.

Aviator makes a number of popular models that come in a variety of sizes. These harnesses feature a self–adjusting elastic leash that allows the bird to fly safely and land without undue restraint.

It's important to practice with your pet inside several times to make sure you know how to attach the harness properly and securely. The first time you venture outside with your macaw, the bird may be a little overwhelmed and frightened. Start in a quiet location so the bird is less likely to be startled and panic.

As you both get used to the harness, you'll want to teach your pet to fly to you on command the same way you taught the bird to "step up".

This will help you to retrieve the macaw more easily, and show your bird that coming to you during harness outings means it's safe and protected.

Bird harnesses are priced from $30 to $50 / £19.50 to £32.50.

Travel Carrier

Travel carriers, also called travel crates, are used exactly as the name implies. They are a temporary means of confining your pet for its own safety. You will need a unit large enough for the macaw to sit comfortably without damaging its tail feathers.

Scarlet Macaws are, on average about 32" / 81.3 cm long, so the travel crate you select should be at least that tall. Many of these units collapse for easy storage when not in use. They are priced in a range of $100 to $150 / £65 to £97.50.

Time Away from Your Parrot

All pet owners face one common concern: What happens when it is time to go on vacation? Many people travel with their pets, but the fact is pets cannot always go with their families. What will you do with your bird when you have to go away from home – on vacation or out of town for business or for a funeral, for example?

Consider who will watch your bird before the need ever arises. You have several options. Perhaps a friend or a family member, who has been around your bird and feels comfortable, can bring him home to care for him.

Pet sitters are also a popular option, especially in the United States where pet sitting businesses must be licensed and insured to operate. A pet sitter generally comes to your home to visit your pet – to ensure he has food, water, and time out to exercise. Pet sitters typically charge per visit, and you can schedule several visits each day.

Is a pet sitter a viable option for your bird? That depends. How long will you be gone? Can you afford to have the pet

Chapter 6: Daily Care

sitter come several times each day to ensure your bird will get time out of his cage? Be sure, if you look for a pet sitter, to find someone who has experience caring for birds or who is willing to take the time to learn about macaws and their care. Before you hire a pet sitter or agree to a visiting schedule, the pet sitter will generally come to your home for an initial consultation. During that meeting, you will talk with the pet sitter about your bird, his schedule, his diet, and how often he requires a visit each day. But, more importantly, the meeting will allow your bird and the pet sitter to meet and to become comfortable around each other. Some pet sitters charge for this initial meeting, but many do not.

You can find pet sitters in the United States through the National Association of Pet Sitters (www.petsitters.org) and Pet Sitters International (www.petsit.com). A comprehensive list of pet sitters in the United Kingdom can be found through the National Association of Registered Pet Sitters (www.dogsit.com) and yes, they look after more than dogs!

Make sure that your pet sitter is insured and fully referenced as they will have access to you home and your pet. You should also contact your home insurance providers to confirm your cover is not affected by having a pet sitter stay at your home.

If you do not like the idea of a pet sitter, consider contacting your local parrot or large bird rescue. Some rescue organizations offer boarding and pet sitting services while others may just be able to provide you with recommendations of sitters.

The North American Parrot Society or the Parrot Society of the UK – or local bird groups – may also have members who offer to pet sit macaws while their owners are on vacation.

If you do the footwork by asking friends, investigating pet sitters, and talking with local bird groups, then you should have little trouble finding a knowledgeable person to watch your bird for you.

Coming Home Again

How will your parrot react when you return home, especially if you have been gone a considerable period? Well, birds are like people, so do not be surprised if your beloved friend is angry with you for having left him. And, like people, he will need time to shed that anger.

Be gentle with your parrot, talking to him and treating him like normal, so he can become reassured that everything is okay. Do not become overly aggressive with him or push him to adjust to his normal life. Doing so could backfire, and your bird may need even more time to get back to normal.

Chapter 7: Quick Facts on Behavior

For the most part, Scarlet Macaws are flexible and quite easy companion animals. They very much enjoy interaction with their humans, but when well-adjusted and provided with adequate toys and means of intellectual stimulation, they'll get along fine on their own while you're at work.

They do however love being part of the family and will quickly pick up on routines and aspects of your lifestyle and are eager to be a part of what's going on.

Chapter 7: Quick Facts on Behavior

Generally, if a Scarlet Macaw acts out, it's either trying to send you a message, or it's engaging in negative behaviors you have unwittingly reinforced.

Problem Behaviors

When Scarlet Macaws "act out," this is not an instance of having a "bad bird" on your hands, but rather a pet that is trying to get a message across.

The typical behavior problems seen in pet birds of all types include:

- biting and other acts of aggression
- screaming or squawking loudly for no reason
- feather plucking

Basically, your Scarlet Macaw is stuffing the "complaint box" with issues you're not addressing to the bird's satisfaction. These likely include:

- "This cage is too small for me!"
- "Get me out of here. I want to fly around!"
- "I'm so bored I could scream. So I will!"
- "I don't like what's happening or I'm scared!"

Chapter 7: Quick Facts on Behavior

It's also possible that your macaw is quite simply just angry for no particular reason. This is especially true of younger birds experiencing hormonal mood swings. The "teenage" years aren't pretty, regardless of species.

Learn to Read Body Language

It really doesn't take much insight to figure out what kind of mood your macaw is in at the moment. A happy, contented pet may give you a little friendly, inquisitive nip, but a bird with flashing eyes and puffed out feathers is looking to take a hunk out of someone.

Watch your macaw's face. The bare facial area, which is normally white, will flush pink when your bird's mood changes.

When you detect obvious signs of ill temper or aggression, leave your pet alone! Give the macaw time to calm down, including time alone in a bird safe room to fly around and work off its mood.

Don't Retaliate

If your bird screams at you and you scream back, the neighbors are going to be in for quite a verbal sparring match, but the exercise will get you nowhere.

Ignore squawking and screaming. When the bird quietens down, be generous with both your praise and affection. Reward and/or reinforce only the kind of behaviors you want to see in your macaw.

Never exhibit aggressive reactions like splashing your bird with water or giving is a disciplinary swat. Aggression begets aggression. If you want your bird to calm down, be calm toward the bird. If there's nothing else to do but back off, then back off.

Push Back Appropriately

A Scarlet Macaw or any other kind of pet is perfectly capable of seizing the upper hand if they realize they're winning. If your bird bites you and you draw back your hand with a yelp, the macaw will realize that it's "won" that round.

Even if you are in pain, control your reactions when your bird bites, and gently push your hand toward your pet. Macaws are smart. When an action like biting doesn't get them the reaction they've come to expect, they will change their behavior.

Preening

Birds are very tidy creatures. They spend a lot of time cleaning their feathers to stay well insulated, waterproof, and in prime flight condition.

Your macaw will use its beak to remove debris and spread beneficial oils throughout its plumage. It's common to see a bird preen after a bath or a meal.

If you are housing a pair of macaws, the birds will preen one another. For that matter, your Scarlet Macaw may well preen you, gently running its beak through your hair. Although this is likely to tickle, let the bird do it! Preening is a huge compliment and an expression of just how much your macaw loves you.

Chapter 7: Quick Facts on Behavior

Other Common Behaviors

Other behaviors common to birds include:

- eye pinning: When the bird becomes excited, the pupils of the eyes will dilate in and out. This would not be a good time to stick your hand in the cage.

- tail flaring: This is also an indication of an excited state. The bird flares its tail feathers out into a fan. Tail flaring and eye pinning often happen concurrently.

- wing flapping: Your macaw may sit on its perch and flap its wings as if it's about to take off in flight. This is a sign of being in a good mood and just wanting a little exercise.

Chapter 7: Quick Facts on Behavior

Beak grinding and wiping are perfectly normally, and you may see your macaw bobbing its head indicating it is anxious to go somewhere — likely wherever you are.

Remember, your bird is an individual, and can display all kinds of behavioral quirks that are uniquely its own.

The more time you spend with your macaw, the better you will be able to read your pet's body language and understand what the macaw is trying to say.

Of course, the advantage of living with a vocal and smart bird like a Scarlet Macaw is that your pet may just come right out and say what it has to say!

Chapter 8: Health

Although Scarlet Macaws are large birds, they will try to hide symptoms of illness in an effort not to appear vulnerable to attack due to their weakened condition.

Part of your responsibility as a macaw owner is to act as a preventive health "plan". Simply by observing your bird, handling your pet, and interacting with it daily, you can quickly spot signs of illness and address them before a health crisis occurs.

Chapter 8: Health

Signs of a Sick Bird

You will always be the best preventive health care your Scarlet Macaw can depend on. Over time, you will come to know your bird intimately. If you think something is wrong, listen to your gut and have the bird evaluated by an avian veterinarian.

You should never wait to seek medical attention for a companion bird. Even a big, hardy bird like a Scarlet Macaw can sicken and die quickly.

Signs you should watch for include:

- Swelling in and around the beak, or any accumulations that might indicate the presence of a mass or an abscess.

- Respiratory difficulties, in particular wheezing or coughing.

- Discharge from the eyes or the nose. There are two air holes or nares just above the beak. Look for discharge in this area.

- Redness or swelling of the eyes.

- Feathers that are missing, soiled, or fluffed out for a prolonged period of time.

- Stools that are overly liquid in nature or that are discolored.

Chapter 8: Health

- Sitting on the floor of the cage. This is not normal behavior and is a sure sign of illness.

- Favoring one foot over the other or the refusal to use one foot for its normal purpose. Scarlet Macaws tend to eat with the left foot and support themselves with the right.

- Loss of appetite.

Although all of these markers can be an indicator of illness, this is not an all–inclusive list. Again, you will know your bird. Listen to your instincts.

Common Health Issues

There are a range of health issues that occur in companion birds of virtually any species. It is imperative that you are on the lookout for any signs of serious illness. Companion birds can fall seriously ill and succumb rapidly without proper medical intervention.

Chlamydiosis

Every year in the United States of America some 100 to 200 cases of chlamydiosis are reported in people who keep parrots, parakeets or budgerigars. This zoonotic disease, also called psittacosis, is caused by the chlamydophila psittaci bacteria. It is also seen in pigeons, doves, cockatiels and cockatoos.

Transmission occurs when the affected bird or human breathes in the dust created by dried fecal materials and nasal secretions. In situations where many birds are housed together, this inhalation can happen easily.

An added complication is the long length of time the highly contagious organism can live outside a host body. It is extremely important that a high level of caution be observed when cleaning cages in which infected birds are housed.

Symptoms in birds include loss of appetite, weight loss, and dehydration. There will be discharge from the eyes and nose, and stools will appear greenish in color. The bird will be lethargic, and sit with feathers fluffed out.

Treatment with doxycycline must begin immediately (orally or as an injection) and should continue for 45 days.

If the bird survives, it should be tested in a month to determine if it has become a carrier of the disease. Until that time, it must remain isolated from other birds.

Humans with chlamydiosis will feel as if they have a case of the flu. If untreated, however, the disease is fatal in 15 to 20% of cases.

Chlamydiosis or psittacosis must be reported to the U.S. Department of Agriculture and/or the local public health department and to the Department of Health in the UK.

Diarrhea

Companion birds are subject to bouts of diarrhea from many sources, but the major culprits are:

- changes in diet
- the presence of internal parasites
- stress

Typically you will see evidence not only of loose stools, but also weight loss and a ruffling of the feathers.

Chapter 8: Health

Over-the-counter medications like Lamber Kay Pet Pectillin can be used to treat the problem. Cost: $7 / £4.55

Do not, however, allow your macaw to go through an extended episode of diarrhea without seeking the advice of a qualified veterinary professional.

Feather Plucking

Birds that pluck their own feathers are most often expressing boredom, depression and loneliness. Some amount of feather loss is just a natural consequence of grooming, but bald patches (especially those that show signs of bleeding) are not normal.

Feather loss can also be a sign of more serious conditions like:

- skin inflammation
- dry skin
- an allergic reaction
- feather cyst disease
- liver disease
- malnutrition

It's also possible that your bird just isn't getting enough fresh air and sunlight. Try to judge your pet's overall condition. Show the macaw more attention, and increase its level of intellectual stimulation.

If you do not see improvement in the feather plucking behavior fairly quickly, seek the advice and aid of an avian veterinarian.

Arthritis in Older Birds

Due to their longevity, Scarlet Macaws can develop arthritis feet. Making sure they have an adequate number of perches to exercise on while in their cages can help to prevent this condition, or to slow its progression.

As a bird develops arthritis, its toes may become disfigured, pointing in unnatural directions just as a human's fingers would show the effects of this degenerative disease.

The macaw may show a marked change in mood, snapping at its feet in an attempt to "drive away" the pain since the bird can only interpret the sensation as something "attacking" it. Depending on the severity of the condition, the macaw may not be able to move around easily while perching, or may appear to be clumsy or even "drunk".

Consult with an avian veterinarian for the best course of action, which may include the use of anti–inflammatory agents, alteration of the diameter of available perches, or even the introduction of a heat source.

Scaly Face and Leg Disease

If you see white deposits on the macaw's legs and feet, or near the beak and eyes, your bird may have become infested with mites.

This condition must be addressed quickly with oral or injected anti–parasitic medications to prevent potential deformations of the beak and legs.

Aspergillosis

A fungus causes the respiratory illness aspergillosis, which is most often seen in stressed birds housed in poor conditions. It is a difficult condition to diagnose and is often well advanced upon detection.

Treatment is individually tailored, so the aid of a veterinarian is crucial. If your bird is kept in a well-ventilated, clean, well-lit environment, the risk of aspergillosis should be quite minimal.

Candidiasis

White lesions on the bird's mouth and throat could be an indication of on overgrowth of yeast in the digestive tract resulting in a candidiasis infection.

Additionally, the bird will have a depressed appetite and will vomit. An anti-fungal medication obtained from an avian veterinarian should address the problem.

Pacheco's Disease

Unfortunately, this condition is almost always fatal and is rarely detected in time for any treatment to be attempted. Pacheco's Disease is caused by a group of herpes viruses and is spread through feces, food and water.

There are more than 130 types of herpes viruses that trigger illnesses in a host of species. The herpes virus is normally host specific and the virus that affects humans is not known to affect psittacine birds or vice versa.

The affected bird will excrete green feces, have little to no appetite, appear listless and may tremble. There will be redness around the eyes and the feathers will likely appear ruffled. The infection primarily attacks the spleen, liver and kidneys.

If the bird survives, it will be a carrier of Pacheco's Disease for the rest of its life and cannot be kept with any other birds.

Proventricular Dilation Disease (PDD)

Also known as Parrot Wasting Syndrome, Proventricular Dilation Disease causes weight loss, vomiting, swelling of the crop and changes in the feces.

Some affected birds can survive for many months with Proventricular Dilation Disease if they receive veterinary support, but there is no treatment or cure for this disease, and it is ultimately fatal.

Parrot Allergies in Humans

When any bird preens, flaps its wings, or defecates, dander and debris are spread in the immediate area.

If oil is present in the dander, the material will adhere to surfaces. If it is dusty, the dander spreads widely. Thus, it's almost impossible for a person with an allergic sensitivity to really avoid the substance.

Asthmatics will be especially susceptible to a negative reaction, but anyone with an allergic sensitivity may find themselves with itchy, watery eyes. Skin irritations are also common, as is severe respiratory distress.

It is helpful if the bird's cage is cleaned daily and vacuums equipped with HEPA filters are used, but even for people experiencing a mild allergic reaction, it may not be practical to live with a companion bird.

Protein present in the dander is the root cause of the reaction, but the proteins vary by species. A person who is allergic to a dog or cat may not be allergic to a bird.

It is sensible however, considering the many years you will spend with your macaw, to be tested for potential sensitivity to bird dander before adopting a Scarlet Macaw.

Dander Pneumoconiosis

Working in close proximity to birds increases the level of exposure to avian dander, a problem especially prevalent in breeders or enthusiasts who maintain large aviaries. In rare cases, humans can contract Dander Pneumoconiosis, which is also called Alveolitis.

This respiratory condition causes a reduction of lung capacity due to damage to the inner lining of the lungs, the alveoli. Please note, however, that it may be 10 to 20 years before a person becomes symptomatic.

When pneumoconiosis becomes acute, it presents with coughing and chills, labored breathing and a high fever. In the sub-acute stage, the person will suffer from a dry cough that gradually becomes persistent.

It's quite easy to simply ignore early-stage pneumoconiosis and to assume the cough is a consequence of seasonal allergies or sinus problems.

If high levels of dander exposure continue in the absence of any breathing protection, like the use of protective masks, the damage to the lungs may be permanent.

Although rare, it is possible for pneumoconiosis to progress to a life-threatening illness like pulmonary fibrosis.

Special Note: Avian Flu

In 2003, birds tested in Asia, Europe, and Africa were found to have the H5N1 Avian Influenza virus, a deadly zoonotic disease. Humans who come into contact with the fecal matter of infected birds can contract the virus.

It must be emphasized, however, that at the time of writing, H5N1 is a problem only in poultry and fowl kept in crowded, often deplorable conditions. The disease has not been linked to companion birds.

In the interest of full disclosure, however, it is possible for any species of bird to be infected with H5N1. The status of this emerging pathogen is being carefully monitored by health agencies around the world.

As with any emerging pathogen, H5N1 is being closely monitored by health agencies around the world and cannot be completely dismissed in relation to any bird species. It would be advisable to check the up to date position before buying your companion bird.

We have briefly looked at Parrot Allergies in Humans, Dander Pneumoconiosis and Avian Flu. Before making the decision to bring a companion bird into your life, we strongly recommend that you take advice from your doctor and veterinarian so that you have a full understanding of any risks to your own health.

Chapter 9: Veterinary Care

Scarlet macaws can live well into their seventh decade. But, for a macaw to live to a ripe old age, he must be cared for properly. That means finding a qualified, experienced avian vet to care for your parrot, both when he is sick and for annual check-ups.

General veterinarians typically have extensive knowledge of dogs and cats and may have little to no experience with birds. As a result, unless you absolutely have no other choice, such as during an emergency, you should avoid going to a veterinarian who does not specialize in birds.

Be forewarned that with that specialized knowledge that your avian vet will provide you and your bird, you will generally pay significantly more in vet fees and this is one reason why it is important to research before choosing the best avian vet for you and for your macaw.

In this section, we are going to discuss how to find a qualified avian vet.

Finding a Vet

Ask other parrot owners for recommendations.

Sometimes the best way to find a great avian vet is to ask others who own macaws and parrots. If you do not know someone in your neighborhood with a bird, contact your local avian rescue or go online and find an online discussion group in your area and start asking for recommendations. In addition to helping you find a good, qualified vet, other parrot owners can help you avoid the not-so-desirable avian vets.

Ask plenty of questions as to why the person recommends the particular vet. Is the vet personable and knowledgeable about parrots in general? Does he have experience? Are his prices reasonable, in the person's opinion? Find out as much as you can as to why the person likes the avian vet. Also ask him what he does not like about the avian vet.

Chapter 9: Veterinary Care

Use a referral resource.

Check out the Association of Avian Veterinarians (www.aav.org) in the United States of America for an avian vet near you or contact your state's Veterinary Medical Association. In the United Kingdom check out the Vet Index Directory for bird and exotics at: - (www.vetindex.co.uk/vetindex/avian_ref.htm). In Europe, the best source of information is the European Association of Avian Veterinarians at www.EAAVonline.org

The websites provide comprehensive lists of avian vets, which can put you on the right track to find a qualified vet near you.

Call local veterinarians to determine if they have experience with birds.

Avian vets generally advertise themselves as such and generally see either only birds or birds and other exotics, such as house rabbits and small animals. If you decide to call local veterinarians, do not ask the receptionist, or whoever answers the phone, if the vet deals with birds. Instead, ask "What kind of pets do the veterinarians at the practice care for?" You are much more likely to get an honest answer that way. If you ask, "does the vet see birds?" the receptionist may very well respond yes, even though that veterinarian may specializes in dogs and cats and has only cared for a bird once or twice in an emergency situation.

Chapter 9: Veterinary Care

Interview Potential Avian Vets

You are investing a great deal, both financially and emotionally, in your Scarlet Macaw. So, you really want to make sure he gets the best veterinary care possible.

That means finding a qualified, experienced avian vet. Before you choose a veterinarian, interview several then decide who the best vet is for you and your bird. It would be wise to find a suitable vet before you bring your macaw home to ensure that you have access to a specialist vet in your area.

Call and make an appointment with the veterinarian, explaining to the receptionist that you need an avian vet and would like to meet the vet and discuss his philosophy on caring for parrots and so on.

At the appointment, be sure to ask plenty of questions, such as:

- How many Scarlet Macaws do you see in a month? In a year?

- How many parrots do you typically see in a month? In a year?

- How long have you worked with birds?

- Are you certified by the American Board of Veterinary Practitioners (if in the United States)?

Chapter 9: Veterinary Care

- Do you have emergency hours? If not, can you recommend an avian vet who does have emergency hours?

- Do you make house calls?

- Do you recommend annual exams? If so, of what do the annual exams consist?

- What kind of continuing education do you participate in to stay up to date with the latest treatments for illnesses and diseases in parrots?

- What is the fee for a typical annual exam? What is the fee for an emergency visit? If you make house calls, how much do you charge and how do they work i.e. under what circumstances do you make house calls?

- Does your veterinary practice accept pet insurance (we will discuss pet insurance later in the book)?

- What are the risks to my own health when owning a Scarlet Macaw?

As mentioned in Chapters three and eight, before making the decision to bring a companion bird into your life, we strongly recommend that you take advice from your doctor and veterinarian so that you have a full understanding of any risks to your own health.

Ask as many questions as you need to feel comfortable about making a decision on whether or not you have found the right vet. Write down the questions before you go, so you do not forget to ask anything that is important to you.

After you have found a vet you think is the right fit, schedule a well visit for your bird. The well visit will allow you to see the avian vet in action and to determine if you made the right choice.

During that initial visit, pay careful attention. Is your bird at ease? Does the vet seem interested and knowledgeable? Do you feel comfortable with how the vet is treating your bird and with his level of knowledge?

Both you and your Scarlet Macaw should feel comfortable and you should feel confident in your chosen avian vet's ability to care for your bird.

What happens in an emergency?

You are likely going to face one major challenge when searching for an avian vet: Finding a vet who has emergency hours. Emergency vets and emergency veterinary clinics in many cities focus predominately on dogs and cats. Some may have a vet on staff that is familiar with birds or other exotics, but most bird and exotic owners find it difficult to find an emergency vet who specializes in their particular pet.

Chapter 9: Veterinary Care

Please bear in mind that you may have difficulty finding an emergency vet, so it makes sense to find one before you ever face an emergency. The last thing you want is to lose precious time searching for a qualified vet when your bird is sick or injured or to take him to a vet who is not qualified and who compounds the problem instead of helping to fix it.

Typical vets costs each year

How much you can expect to pay in veterinary costs each year really depends upon the health of your Scarlet Macaw and how much your avian vet charges for visits, blood work, X-rays, and any other care your bird may need. It also depends upon where you live. You will likely pay less in smaller cities than in a large metropolitan area.

Your best bet for determining your estimated annual veterinary expenses for your parrot is to call around and get pricing from the avian veterinarians in your area.

Get estimates for annual check-ups, any tests required, costs of vaccinations and what emergency call out fees would be before you bring your bird home so you know whether you can realistically afford to care for him, including if he becomes ill.

Annual Exam

Even if your macaw appears to be healthy and happy, he needs to have an annual exam with his avian veterinarian every year. Ask your avian vet what he includes in a typical annual exam.

An annual exam may consist of:

- A full physical exam
- Weight check
- Testing of droppings
- Blood work
- Testing for viruses
- Any necessary vaccinations

The annual exam is the ideal time to ask the avian veterinarian any general questions you may have about your bird. However, you should not wait until the annual exam if you have any concerns that could affect your bird's health.

Pet Insurance

Veterinary care, especially for birds, can become quite pricey. In addition to the fact that avian vets generally come with a higher price tag, you never know when an illness or

Chapter 9: Veterinary Care

injury will occur, resulting in expensive and unexpected costs.

With advances in veterinary care, today's pets can receive the same high quality care – such as chemotherapy for cancer and physical therapy for injuries – as their human counterparts. The cost of that care, however, can become quite hefty, making it essential for you to know how you plan to pay for veterinary care even before you bring your bird home.

Many pet owners have discovered that pet insurance helps defray the costs of veterinary expenses. Pet insurance is similar to health insurance in that you pay a monthly premium and a deductible (excess in the UK) and the pet insurance pays for whatever is covered in your plan, such as annual exams and blood work.

Chapter 9: Veterinary Care

Shopping for pet insurance is similar to shopping for health insurance in the United States. As with health insurance, the age and the overall health of your Scarlet Macaw will determine how much you will pay in premiums and deductibles. Ask plenty of questions to determine the best company and plan for your needs:

- Can you go to your regular vet, or do you have to go to a vet assigned by the pet insurance company?

- What does the insurance plan cover? Does it cover annual exams? Surgeries? Emergency illness and injury?

- Does coverage begin immediately?

- Are pre–existing conditions covered? In addition, if your macaw develops a health issue and you later have to renew the policy, is that condition covered when you renew your policy?

- Is medication covered?

- Do you have to have pre–authorization before your pet receives treatment? What happens if your bird has the treatment without pre–authorization?

- Does the insurance policy cover dental issues and chronic health problems, including arthritis, the latter of which Scarlet Macaws are prone?

Chapter 9: Veterinary Care

- Is there a lifetime maximum benefit amount? If so, how much is that amount? A benefit plan with a lifetime maximum of only a few hundred dollars surely will not suffice for a parrot (or most pets, for that matter).

- Is there an amount that you have to pay before the insurance pays out?

Take the time to research your pet insurance options. Compare the different plans available, what each covers, and the cost before making the decision on which is best for you and your pet.

Pet insurance may not be the answer for everyone. While it may not be a feasible option for you, consider having a backup plan, just in case your bird requires emergency care or you run into unexpected veterinarian costs.

A simple way to prepare for an emergency is to start a veterinary fund for your Scarlet Macaw. Decide to put a certain amount of money aside each week, each month, or each pay–check to use in the case of an emergency. Think about the potential financial costs of veterinary care and plan for how you will pay for it now instead of waiting until something happens.

Chapter 10: Scarlet Macaw Care Sheet

With proper care, Scarlet Macaws can live to age 75 or more in captivity. In this chapter we provide a care sheet giving a summary of what we have discussed so far.

Housing and Habitat

Recommended minimum cage size:
2.5' wide x 4' deep x 5' tall / 0.76m x 1.22m x 1.52m with bars spacing no greater than 1 inch / 2.54 cm.

The standard rule of thumb with any bird is to buy the largest cage you can afford and accommodate in your home.

The cage should include a variety of perches to encourage exercise, and be outfitted with a pan at the bottom to capture excrement and cast off food.

Opt for a stainless steel cage, and make sure any hard plastic elements are BPA and PVC free.

Positioning the Cage

Pick a well-travelled area. Do not place the cage in front of a window, or where the bird will be subject to a draft. Remember, Scarlet Macaws are perfectly happy at average room temperatures, but do not allow their area to reach 80 F/ 26.7 C or higher.

Macaws like their cage to be against one solid wall as it gives them a greater sense of security.

Remember, however, that Scarlet Macaws are highly social creatures. They like to be able to see what's going on, and don't be surprised if they have an opinion about everything!

Chapter 10: Scarlet Macaw Care Sheet

Cage Maintenance

Clean your macaw's cage daily, removing and discarding the soiled liner in the dropping tray. Also remove any feces that have accumulated inside the cage.

Take advantage of the time your bird is enjoying its free flight time and wash the cage components on a weekly basis with warm, soapy water. Make sure you rinse thoroughly and ensure everything is dried properly before returning your macaw to its cage.

On a monthly basis, take the cage completely apart, and if necessary take it outside to be thoroughly hosed off.

The pressure of the hose will help to dislodge any debris that has become stuck, and the fresh air and sunlight are useful in controlling odors.

Use vinegar and baking soda, which are natural disinfectants to clean the various parts. Ensure you rinse thoroughly. Never use any household chemicals on your bird's home.

These substances can be toxic to your pet, even if they are present as residue only.

Remember, Macaws like to chew, so you have to think about what they might come into contact with that could prove harmful to them.

Chapter 10: Scarlet Macaw Care Sheet

Chew Toys

Scarlet Macaws are vigorous and efficient chewers. Choose extra–large chew toys and provide a steady supply for your pet inside and outside of its cage.

Diet and Nutrition

Sixty to seventy percent of your bird's diet should be comprised of a well–balanced pellet food. Use seeds sparingly, as the fat content is too high.

Your bird should have a constant supply of clean, de–chlorinated water. Provide fresh water daily.

Chapter 10: Scarlet Macaw Care Sheet

Appropriate fresh fruits and vegetables include:

- apples
- pears
- berries
- grapes
- mango
- bananas
- figs
- cranberries
- melons
- carrots
- turnips
- yams
- broccoli
- cucumber
- celery
- sweet potatoes
- peppers
- dark green leafy vegetables such as kale

These should be offered daily, with uneaten food removed from the cage within 24 hours.

Do NOT feed your Scarlet Macaw avocados or fruit seeds, or allow your pet to have access to caffeine, alcohol or chocolate.

Chapter 10: Scarlet Macaw Care Sheet

Food and Water Bowls

For macaws, choose at least a 16 fluid ounce / 0.5 liter water bottle with a ball bearing "lixit" tip.

Stainless steel food bowls that can be attached to the side of the cage are recommended. These should have a capacity of at least 20 ounces / 0.57 kgs.

Mineral Supplementation

Like many pet birds, Scarlet Macaws should be provided with a mineral block as a source of calcium and other nutrients.

Grooming

Bathe your Scarlet Macaw regularly in lukewarm, chlorine-free water. Some people prefer to use a grooming spray or to just mist their bird.

Your pet's nails will need to be trimmed, but if possible, have this procedure performed by a veterinarian.

Interaction and Training

Scarlet Macaws are both highly affectionate and extremely intelligent. As you and your bird get to know one another, your interaction will become easy and natural.

Do not be surprised if your bird begins to mimic sounds in its environment, or to repeat phrases it hears you and your family use or things the bird hears on the television.

Cater to the macaw's natural inclinations to teach your pet tricks. The more you handle your bird, the happier your pet will be psychologically and the less difficulty you will have transporting your bird and controlling its behavior indoors.

Never take your bird outside of your home unless your pet is securely placed in a travel carrier or safely attached to a harness as described below.

Bird Harnesses

Bird flight harnesses are an option for additional exercise and interaction with your pet. The harnesses come in a variety of sizes, and feature a self-adjusting elastic leash that allows the bird to fly safely and land without undue restraint.

It is important to practice with your pet to ensure that you have attached the harness properly. The outdoors will initially be a new and potentially frightening experience, so start in a quiet location where your macaw will not become startled or scared.

Teach your macaw to fly to you on command to facilitate retrieval and to help the bird understand that during outings, coming to you means the macaw is safe and protected.

Free Flight Time

Scarlet Macaws need a minimum of two hours of free flight time outside of their cages per day.

The more time your macaw has to exercise and to interact with you, the healthier it will be, physically and psychologically.

Chapter 11: Introduction to Breeding

For the typical Scarlet Macaw owner, breeding is simply not an option due to the enormous requirements of space, attention, time and expense.

For these reasons, it is best to leave the breeding of large, specialized birds like Scarlet Macaws to professional aviaries that have adequate space and sufficient knowledge to safeguard the welfare of the mated pair and their offspring.

Breeding these beautiful and complex birds is not a matter to be undertaken lightly.

Basic Reproductive Facts

Scarlet Macaws reach sexual maturity at 3 to 4 years of age after which they will breed, on average, every one to two years. There is no specific mating season.

Females lay 2 to 4 eggs with an incubation period of 24 to 25 days. The chicks do not reach full independence for 1 to 2 years during which time they remain with their parents.

Both males and females are involved in caring for the young, although males often take the lead in feeding the chicks. The parents will not mate again until their existing offspring can survive on their own.

Mate for Life

Scarlet Macaws present a unique problem when the issue of breeding is raised. The birds form life–long, monogamous relationships with their mates. You must carefully consider the implications of this fact:

- It is cruel to consider separating mated pairs. Separated birds have been known to grieve themselves to death.

- Male Scarlet Macaws cannot be used for stud services. They will not mate with another female.

If you mate a pair of Scarlet Macaws, you are committing yourself to their maintenance for life, including their normal cycle of breeding and producing offspring.

Helpless Chicks

Scarlet Macaw babies are not born without down, and they cannot eat on their own, a state ornithologists call "altricial". The babies will be completely helpless and require months of care from their parents and from you.

If you are planning on selling the chicks, this is not a "fast turnaround" endeavor. During that time, you will be caring for the needs and meeting the expenses of multiple birds.

Establishing a Breeding Pair

Should you decide to undertake the breeding of your Scarlet Macaws, you must be certain that you have adequate room, time and support for the endeavor. You will have to find a good quality male or female, and allow the birds to form a bond on their own.

If you are buying a pair of Scarlet Macaws together, you should be aware of the following terms:

proven pair – The birds have produced eggs or raised young at some time in their lives.

producing pair – The birds have recently produced eggs or raised young.

bonded pair – The birds appear to be compatible and bonded, but they have not yet produced eggs or young.

A proven or producing pair will be far more expensive than a bonded pair.

Chapter 11: Introduction to Breeding

Large Enclosure Required

For breeding purposes, you will need to house your macaws in an aviary that is no smaller than 8' x 8' x 12' (2.44m x 2.44m x 3.66m) and includes a shelter area 4' x 8' x 4' (1.22m x 2.44m x 1.22m). In truth, however, a larger enclosure would be far more preferable for your comfort and the health of your birds.

Final Observations

I appreciate that this introduction to breeding is a very general and brief synopsis. I feel very strongly that for most owners it is a step that requires considered reflection and a lot more in debt advice and guidance than I can provide in this book.

If it is something you would like to investigate further, then the best advice I can give is to seek out a breeder who is willing to share and pass on their experience. Taking the plunge and hoping for the best is not the approach to adopt and you must consider the time, cost, facilities and resources required to manage breeding successfully along with the impact on you and your family.

Chapter 11: Introduction to Breeding

Scarlet Macaws

Chapter 12: Life after You

Sometimes life takes unexpected turns. If you have ever volunteered at or have been to an animal shelter, you have likely heard the heartbreaking stories of some of the homeless dogs, cats, birds, rabbits and other animals.

Their beloved human has passed away and they are now at the shelter, confused and depressed. Countless pets languish in animal shelters and rescues after their owner dies because the person failed to make plans for their pet's future without them.

Chapter 12: Life after You

Most people expect to outlive their pets by many years. But, that does not always happen. What will happen to your parrot once you are gone? Scarlet Macaws have a much longer lifespan than most pets, so that is a question you really want to think about and answer now. If something happens to you, you want to know that your bird will be properly cared for and loved.

Some cell phones allow you to input an ICE (In Case of Emergency) number with notes. If your cell phone has such an option, I recommend that you use it. Alternatively, you might find it easier to write the following information on a piece of a paper and put it in your wallet with your driver's license. You can also give a copy of this information to your neighbors along with friends and family. The list should include:

- The names of each of your pets, including your Scarlet Macaw

- The names and phone numbers of family members or friends who have agreed to temporarily care for your pets in an emergency.

The name and phone number of your avian veterinarian and other vets if you have other pets.

Be sure to also talk with your neighbors, letting them know how many pets you have and the type of pets. That way, if something happens to you, they can alert the authorities, ensuring your pets do not linger for days before they are found.

Chapter 12: Life after You

If you fail to do that and something happens to you, someone will find your pet and will have questions: What is his name? What does he eat? How old is he? To make sure your bird is not forgotten in the case of an emergency, ask several friends or family members to be responsible for taking care of him temporarily should something happen to you.

Even before something happens, prepare instructions for the intended temporary guardians, providing amended instructions as necessary. Also, if you are happy to do so, provide each individual with a key to your home. Remember to let your home insurer know you have done and ask them to confirm that does not affect your coverage.

Instructions to the guardians should include:

- The name and phone numbers of each individual who agreed to temporarily take care of your parrot and other pets.

- Your Scarlet Macaws diet and feeding schedule, so he can maintain his normal schedule.

The name and phone number of your avian veterinarian

- Any health problems and medications your bird may take on a daily basis, including dosage instructions, instructions on how to give the medicine, and where the medicine is kept.

- Information on the care of your parrot, such as when he typically sleeps, how much time he generally gets out of the cage and so on.

Put as much information as necessary to ensure the temporary guardians can provide the same level of care to which your Scarlet Macaw is accustomed.

Finding a Permanent Home for Your Macaw

Ensure your bird's future by finding a permanent home for him in case of your unexpected incapacity or death. Here are some things to keep in mind when considering a new home for your beloved friend in the event of your death:

- Consider family members and friends who love animals and have successfully cared for pets themselves. You may have a particular family member, for example, who is fond of your Scarlet Macaw and vice-versa.

- How many pets do you have? If you have a pair of Scarlet Macaws, do not split them up if at all possible. Breaking up a pair could result in great distress, including self-mutilation, feather plucking, screaming and even death.

- Is the person you are considering willing to care for a parrot, regardless of how long he lives? He may even outlive his new guardian.

Chapter 12: Life after You

- Find an alternate new guardian in case something happens and the first one is unable to care for your pet as intended.

- Always remain in contact with the potential new guardian to ensure he or she is still able or willing to care for your bird (and other pets) in case of an emergency. If one person backs out, you can then take the time necessary to find another potentially permanent guardian.

Making it Legal

Once you have found the best caregiver, consult with a lawyer or a solicitor. The lawyer/solicitor can create a legal agreement, whether a will or a trust, that is based on what you want for your pet in the case of your unexpected death.

A will can dictate who your bird is to live with upon your death while you can place funds – to help pay for the ongoing care of your Scarlet Macaw – in a trust that the guardian can use to help care for him.

Another alternative is to take out a suitable life insurance policy which can be written under trust to cover your pet's ongoing costs. This is a complex area and I recommend you take specialist advice.

While it is not the most pleasant topic to talk or to think about it, it is extremely important to your pet's continued well–being that you address what is to happen to it and who will take care of it before that time comes.

Chapter 13: Closing Thoughts

The popularity of parrots as companion birds is undeniable, but less commonly known than the popularity of dogs and cats.

Chapter 13: Closing Thoughts

In the United States of America alone there are more than 40 million of these magnificent birds living in homes and enriching the lives of their keepers.

Parrots come in all sizes and colors. They are all vivid tropical birds known for their high level of intelligence. The Scarlet Macaw is one of the largest of the parrots and one of the most popular species kept as a pet.

At best guess, a parrot has an intelligence on par with that of a child between the ages of 3 and 5, but most parrot owners will tell you that should read "child prodigy".

Amazing their owners seems to be a natural pastime for these birds and especially for Scarlet Macaws. Their insight and understanding of what is going on around them can be almost uncanny.

"Scarlets" as they are known in the bird fancy are highly affectionate creatures — so much so that they are often referred to as cuddly. Prospective owners have to understand that these are monogamous birds that mate for life in the wild.

You will truly be your parrot's significant other, and given the fact that a Scarlet Macaw can live for 75 years, the relationship will be a long one. Don't discount this fact. Responsible parrot owners routinely make provisions for their birds in their wills.

If you've read this far and are not daunted by the cost of a Scarlet Macaw (often more than $1,200 / £780), the size of its cage (at least 5 feet / 1.52 meters tall) and the bird's lifespan

Chapter 13: Closing Thoughts

(typically 60 to 75 years). Then you may well be a good candidate to be a parrot owner.

These are not low maintenance birds. They can be loud. They can be petulant when they don't get enough attention. And if they're mad at you, they can bite. But Scarlet Macaws are also bright, inquisitive, loving, loyal and devoted.

In the introduction I recommended that all prospective parrot owners read Joanna Burger's book "The Parrot Who Owns Me: The Story of a Relationship".

In that book Burger wrote, "Tiko [a Red–Lored Amazon Parrot] has taught me, a sometimes headstrong and often ferociously independent woman, the importance of interdependence, the importance of taking care, and the importance of being cared for".

"It's a necessary part of being human and being connected to the world around us that we realize and acknowledge our vulnerability and the vulnerability of all creatures, and that we act in accord with that knowledge".

Be prepared to learn much more from your Scarlet Macaw than you will teach or "train" them. They are magnificent birds and equally magnificent personalities. If you are up for the challenge, your macaw will literally change your life.

Chapter 13: Closing Thoughts

Chapter 14: Frequently Asked Questions

Although you should read the entire text to fully understand Scarlet Macaws and their care, these are some of the most frequently asked questions concerning this magnificent species.

Chapter 14: Frequently Asked Questions

What should my Scarlet Macaw eat?

Your Scarlet Macaw's diet should be weighted more heavily toward sources of protein. Your best bet is to go with a specially formulated pellet food that will comprise 60% to 70% of the overall food intake.

Be sure to check the ingredients, however, and make sure it also contains beta carotene (the precursor of Vitamin A.) In terms of fresh foods, opt for items such as apples, pears, berries, grapes, mango, bananas, figs, cranberries, melons, carrots, turnips, yams, broccoli, cucumber, celery, sweet potatoes, peppers and dark green leafy vegetables such as kale.

Limit the amount of seeds and nuts. When fed in captivity, these items introduce too much fat into the bird's diet.

What kind of cage should I buy?

With any species of bird, the answer is always the same — the biggest you can afford and place in your home. You have to remember that the Scarlet Macaw is one of the biggest of the parrots.

At the very least, you will need to invest in a cage that is 2.5' wide x 4' deep x 5' tall (0.76m x 1.22m x 1.52m). The larger the cage, the happier and healthier your macaw will be. Make sure the bars on the cage you select are spaced at a distance of no more than 1 inch (2.54 centimeters).

Chapter 14: Frequently Asked Questions

Are Scarlet Macaws loud?

They certainly can be extremely noisy. Depending on what the bird is trying to communicate, its vocalizations can range from a piercing squawk to sort of a humming purr — and anything in between. If you or your neighbors can't tolerate the idea of unpredictable noise levels, don't get a Scarlet Macaw!

Can I teach my Scarlet Macaw to talk?

Many species of macaw are highly adept at mimicking human speech, and the Scarlet Macaw is no exception. You may be surprised to find that your pet will also start imitating sounds in the household as well.

Use predictable vocabulary with your bird as you go about its routine. Tell the bird hello and goodbye. Ask it if it wants a carrot as you're offering it one.

The more you help the bird to associated specific phrases with recognizable items or actions, the faster your pet will learn to speak. Just interact and reinforce. The parrot will do the rest.

What about other kinds of tricks?

Scarlet Macaws are highly intelligent. The bird is capable of learning all kinds of "tricks". Watch the bird and start with whatever it's doing on its own in the way of behaviors and

Chapter 14: Frequently Asked Questions

motions. Look for ways to reinforce those things and incorporate them into desired behaviors and tricks.

If you have a bird that has a habit of lifting one foot, for instance, try to turn that into a wave hello or goodbye, or try to teach the bird to "shake hands" on cue. The same kind of reinforcement can be used for common bird behaviors like head bobbing.

Always reinforce desirable results with praise and a treat. When the bird catches on that there's a game involved to all this, the learning curve will accelerate sharply. Just understand, in the macaw's mind, he's teaching you, not the other way around!

How can I tell if my Scarlet Macaw is getting sick?

Learn the bird's habits and behaviors and observe anything that constitutes a change. Watch its appetite and elimination habits, and look for any sign of things like drainage from the eye and nostrils.

Other warning signs include feather plucking, feather puffing, or sitting on the bottom of the cage. See the Chapter eight on health for a fuller discussion of the signs of illness in your pet.

When will my Scarlet Macaw be most active?

Your pet is diurnal, meaning it's active during the day. In

the wild, Scarlet Macaws gather in the trees at night and sleep in flocks. During the day groups tend to gather at a source of clay, while mated pairs fly and forage together. This species mates for life, so expect your pet to develop a deep bond with you over time as you will be its "significant other".

How long will my Scarlet Macaw live?

A Scarlet Macaw that is being well cared for can easily live to 75 years of age in captivity. It is absolutely crucial that you consider this fact before adopting one and have a plan for who will care for your parrot in the event of your death.

It is quite common for macaw owners to make provisions for their birds in their wills. This is not an eccentricity, but an aspect of a responsible and caring pet owner.

How much work goes into keeping a pet bird?

A lot! Don't think with any species of bird that you're getting a low maintenance pet. This is especially true with a bird the size of a Scarlet Macaw.

You will need to change their food and water daily, removing any uneaten fragments. At minimum, the cage will require a thorough cleaning and disinfecting weekly, with more extensive cleaning monthly.

Your bird will need at least two hours of free flight time per

Chapter 14: Frequently Asked Questions

day in a bird safe room. This means there will be messes to clean up outside the cage.

Also, the Scarlet Macaw is a highly aggressive and efficient chewing machine. Unless you give your pet enough chew toys to keep it entertained, it will be game on with whatever the bird finds on its own!

Additionally, these creatures are intelligent and affectionate. In the wild, they mate for life. Your Scarlet Macaw will need and want your attention.

Failure to interact with your bird on a daily basis will harm its degree of socialization, and can lead to aggression that stems from nothing but loneliness and boredom. Make no mistake, Scarlet Macaws have emotional needs.

I really want a parrot, but I don't think it's a good idea. Is there a way I can support parrot conservation in the wild?

Absolutely. Visit the homepage of the World Parrot Trust at www.parrot.org. This group works on behalf of all kinds of parrots around the world.

Chapter 15: Relevant Websites

When you start looking around the internet it can take some time to track down exactly what you are looking for.

A one-stop shop for all your parrot needs is what is required and the sites below offer you the convenience of pulling together many of the best products from around the web.

Shopping

United States Website

www.tropicalbirdshop.com

United Kingdom Website

www.tropicalbirdshop.co.uk

Chapter 15: Relevant Websites

American Federation of Aviculture

www.afabirds.org

AvianWeb

www.avianweb.com

Avicultural Society of America

www.asabirds.org

Aviculture Society of the United Kingdom

www.avisoc.co.uk

Bird Channel – The Website for Bird Lovers

www.birdchannel.com

Bird Talk Magazine

www.birdtalkmagazine.com

International Association of Avian Trainers and Educators

www.iaate.org

Parrots Magazine

www.parrotmag.com

Parrot Rehabilitation Society

www.parrotsociety.org

Chapter 15: Relevant Websites

Parrot Society of Australia

www.parrotsociety.org.au

Talk Parrots

www.talkparrots.com

World Parrot Trust

www.parrots.org/index.php/encyclopedia/profile/scarlet_macaw

CITES and Parrots

In 1973 the Convention on International Trade in Endangered Species of Wild Fauna and Flora (CITES) was established to combat over–exploitation. Worldwide some 160 countries are signatory partners and have management authority relative to licensing and permits.

In the UK this authority resides with the Department for Environment, Food and Rural Affairs (DEFRA). In the United States, it is held by the U.S. Fish and Wildlife Service.

The following list are birds covered under CITES that are facing the danger of extinction. They can only be traded under very specific certification, and for the hobbyist, the vast majority of offers to purchase any of these species should be regarded as potentially illegal.

For further information regarding CITES and parrots:

In the UK contact:

Department for Environment, Food and Rural Affairs - 0117 372 8749. Open 9 a.m. to 5 p.m. www.defra.gov.uk

Or in the United States of America contact:

U.S. Fish and Wildlife Service, 1-800-344-WILD. Open 8:00 a.m. to 8:00 p.m. Eastern Time, Monday through Friday. www.fws.gov

CITES and Parrots

Endangered Parrot Species:

Amazona arausiaca – Red-necked Amazon

Amazona barbadensis – Yellow-Shouldered Amazon

Amazona brasiliensis – Red-tailed Amazon

Amazona finschi – Lilac-crowned Amazon

Amazona guildingii – St Vincent Amazon

Amazona imperialis – Imperial Amazon

Amazona leucocephala – Cuban Amazon

Amazona ochrocephala auropalliata – Yellow-crowned Amazon

Amazona ochrocephala belizensis – Double Yellow-headed Amazon (Belize)

Amazona ochrocephala caribaea – Double Yellow-headed Amazon (Caribaea)

Amazona ochrocephala oratrix – Double Yellow-headed Amazon

Amazona ochrocephala parvipes – Yellow-naped Amazon

Amazona ochrocephala tresmariae – Double Yellow-headed Amazon (Tres Marias)

Amazona pretrei – Red-spectacled Amazon

Amazona rhodocorytha – Rhodocorytha Amazon

Amazona tucumana – Tucuman Amazon

Amazona versicolor – Saint Lucia Amazon

Amazona vinacea – Vinaceous Amazon

Amazona viridigenalis – Green–cheeked Amazon

Amazona vittata – Puerto Rican Amazon

Anodorhynchus hyacinthinus – Hyacinth macaw

Anodorhynchus leari – Lears macaw

Ara ambigua – Great–green macaw (Buffons)

Ara glaucogularis – Blue–throated macaw

Ara macao – Scarlet Macaw

Ara maracana – Illiger's macaw

Ara militaris – Military macaw

Ara rubrogenys – Red–fronted macaw

Cacatua goffini – Goffins Cockatoo

Cacatua haematuropygia – Red–vented Cockatoo

Cacatua moluccensis – Moluccan Cockatoo

Cacatua sulphurea – Lesser Sulphur–crested Cockatoo

Cacatua sulphurea abbitti – Abbots Lesser Sulphur–crested Cockatoo

Cacatua sulphurea parvula – Lesser Sulphur-crested Cockatoo

Cacatua sulphurea citrinocristata – Citron-crested Cockatoo

Cyanopsitta spixii – Spix's macaw

Cyanoramphus forbesi – Chatham Island yellow-fronted parakeet

Cyanoramphus novaezelandiae – Red-fronted parakeet

Cyclopsitta diophthalma – Coxen Coxen's double-eyed fig parrot

Eos histrio – Red and blue lory

Eunymphicus cornutus – Horned parakeet

Geopsittacus occidentalis – Night parrot

Guarouba guarouba – Golden Conure

Neophema chrysogaster – Orange-bellied parrot

Ognorhynchus icterotis – Yellow-eared parrot

Pezoporus wallicus – Ground parrot

Pionopsitta pileata – Pileated parrot

Probosciger aterrimus – Palm Cockatoo

Propyrruha Couloni (formerly Ara Couloni) – Blue-headed macaw

Propyrruha Maracana (formerly Ara Maracana) – Blue-winged macaw

Psephotus chrysopterygius – Golden-shouldered parrot

Psephotus dissimilis – Hooded parrot

Psephotus pulcherrimus – Paradise parrot

Psittacula echo – Mauritus parakeet

Psittacula krameri (Ghana) – Ring-necked parakeet

Pyrrhura cruentata – Blue-throated parakeet

Rhynchopsitta pachyrhyncha – Thick-billed parrot

Rhynchopsitta terrisi – Maroon-fronted parakeet

Strigops habroptilus – Kakapo

Vini ultramarina – Ultramarine Lorikeet

References

Athan, Mattie Sue. *Guide to Companion Parrot Behavior*. Barron's Educational Series, 1999.

Barcott, Bruce. *The Last Flight of the Scarlet Macaw : One Woman's Fight to Save the World's Most Beautiful Bird*. New York: Random House, 2009.

"The Basics of Living with a Parrot," jamiesparrothelp.wordpress.com/2011/12/16/the-basics-of-living-with-a-parrot/

"Basic Information Sheet for the Macaw," LafeberVet.com, www.lafebervet.com/avian-medicine-list/basic-information-sheets-for-the-macaw/

Burger, Joanna. *The Parrot Who Owns Me: The Story of a Relationship*. Villard. 2001.

Hypersensitivity pneumonitis
http://medical-dictionary.thefreedictionary.com/hypersensitivity+pneumonitis

"Iron Storage Disease / Hemochromatosis". Avian Web. www.avianweb.com/ironstoragedisease.html

Moustaki, Nikki. *Parrots for Dummies*. For Dummies Books. 2005

O'Connor, Rebecca K. "10 Facts About Living with Parrots".

References

Birdchannel.com – the website for bird lovers
www.birdchannel.com/bird-species/find-the-right-bird/facts-about-parrots.aspx

Encyclopedia of Life
http://eol.org/pages/1177962/hierarchy_entries/45714477/details

Pacheco's Disease
http://www.petplace.com/birds/pacheco-s-disease/page2.aspx

Parrot Fever/Psittacosis/ Avian Chlamydiosis
www.cfsph.iastate.edu/Factsheets/pdfs/psittacosis.pdf

"Scarlet Macaw" World Parrot Trust.
www.parrots.org/index.php/encyclopedia/captivestatus/scarlet_macaw/

"Scarlet Macaw Common Problems," BirdTricks.com,
www.birdtricks.com/scarlet-macaw-problems.html

Sweeney, Roger G. *Macaws: Barron's Complete Pet Owner's Manuals.* Barron's Educational Series, 2005.

Glossary

allergy – Negative immune responses in sensitive individuals are triggered by a foreign irritating substance. These reactions are called allergies. Many people experience such a reaction to pet dander, but all such allergies are species specific. A person that is allergic to a cat might have no other animal-related sensitivities. Typical allergic symptoms include watering eyes and sneezing with some type of respiratory distress. Itching is also common.

avian specialist – Any veterinarian trained in the specialized treatment of companion birds.

aviary bird – Birds housed outdoors in secure enclosures. This may be a temporary or full-time habitat solution.

beak – On birds, the upper and lower jaws or mandibles form a structure known as the "beak or "bill". This structure in Scarlet Macaws is strong and prominent since the birds use their beaks to crack hard nuts and seeds.

beaking – Many kinds of parrots engage in beaking, an exploratory behavior. The bird is using its bill to investigate something it finds interesting. Although often mistaken for a precursor to biting or aggression, this is simply an expression of curiosity.

bird fancier's lung – Hypersensitivity pneumonitis is often referred to as "bird fancier's lung". The condition is the response of long-term exposure to bird dander. The primary symptom initially is a dry cough. In the chronic state, the affected person will experience chills and fever, and diminished respiratory capacity. Without treatment, the damage to the lungs will become permanent.

breast – The breast of a bird is positioned just below the animal's throat.

cere – Located just above the beak, the cere is a patch of flesh where a bird's nostrils or nares are located.

crop – Roughly comparable to a sac, the crop on a bird is found between the esophagus and stomach. It processes food through preliminary digestion before the material passes lower into the digestive tract.

crown – The uppermost portion of a bird's head.

ear – In normal, healthy birds, the ears are rarely seen. The structures are simply holes on either side of the head just behind the eyes. Typically they are covered with a layer of fine feathers.

eyes – The eyes of a bird have evolved to be position on either side of the head. This gives the creature a maximum field of vision, which serves as both a protection against predation and a means of locating food.

fear aggression – The behavior that occurs in response to an event that frightens an animal. Triggers include motion or sound, and responses range from biting to flight.

hormonal aggression – Upon reaching sexual maturity, many species of company birds exhibit temporary

Glossary

aggressive behavior related to the hormones surging through their systems. This is the avian equivalent of human adolescence.

learned aggression – Negative behaviors that a bird learns in order to get a desired response are referred to as learned aggression. Essentially, this is an instance of your bird being a brat, and acting out because he knows that in doing so, he can force you to do something he wants.

mantle – The anatomical term used to refer to a bird's back.

nape – The anatomical term used to refer to the back of a bird's neck.

nictating membrane – Sometimes called the "third" eyelid, this semi-transparent membrane passes over the surface of a bird's eye. Its purpose is to clean the eye, and to provide lubrication.

parrot – Tropical birds in the family Psittacidae are commonly called parrots. They are brightly colored, and have hooked, short beaks. Many parrots, including macaws, have the ability to mimic human speech.

parrot fever – Caused by the bacterium Chlamydia psittici, this disease can be passed to humans, and if untreated is fatal in 15 to 20% of cases before the use of antibiotics while properly treated cases are rarely fatal.

primary feathers – All birds have ten primary feathers on the wing that allow the creature to take flight.

rump – The rump of a bird is found beneath the primary

Glossary

flight feathers on the lower back.

secondary feathers – The secondary feathers are located under the primary feathers of the wing and lie closer to the body.

territorial aggression – When any animal displays aggression that is triggered by a perceived threat to an area it regards as its own, the response is said to be "territorial aggression".

training aids – Devices used by humans for the purpose of facilitating the training of any animal, including bird, to display a desired behavior or response.

vent – The vent of a bird is found below the tail and is the area from which the creature defecates. Birds do not urinate.

zoonotic – Diseases that can be transmitted from an animal, including a bird, to a human being are said to be zoonotic in nature.

Index

A

aggression ... 28, 91, 93, 151, 162, 163, 164, 165
Ara macao ... 11, 157
Ara macao cyanoptera ... 13
Ara macao macao ... 13
arthritis ... 59, 103, 104, 119
Aspergillosis ... 105
Association of Avian Veterinarians ... 112
Avian influenza virus ... 108
avian vet/avian vets/ avian veterinarian/avian veterinarians ... 2 10, 30 33, 39, 71, 72, 98, 103, 104, 105, 110, 111, 112, 113, 114, 115, 116, 117, 137, 138
aviary/aviaries .. 1, 12, 26, 30, 32, 34, 39, 40, 47, 48, 62, 64, 65, 78, 107, 131, 134, 162
aviculture ... 1

B

baking soda ... 62, 123
beak/beaks ... 1, 2, 13, 14, 15, 25, 33, 38, 49, 52, 94, 96, 98, 104, 162, 163, 164
bird proof/bird proofing ... 51, 52, 56, 57, 67
BPA ... 60, 67, 122
breeder/breeders ... 10, 12, 19, 21, 30, 31, 33, 34, 35, 39, 47, 69, 71, 78, 107, 134
breeding ... 16, 130, 131, 132, 134

C

cage/cages ... 1, 6, 24, 25, 27, 30, 37, 50, 51, 52, 53, 55, 57, 59, 60, 61, 62, 63, 64, 66, 72, 73, 75, 76, 79, 83, 88, 91, 95, 99, 100, 103, 107, 122, 123, 124, 125, 127, 129, 139, 143, 147, 149, 150, 151
calcium ... 2, 74, 127
Candidiasis ... 105
captivity ... 12, 13, 16, 18, 74, 121, 147, 150
chew toy/chew toys ... 2, 25, 38, 49, 52, 67, 74, 124, 151
chicks ... 2, 131, 132
Chlamydiosis ... 100, 101

Index

CITES...12, 155
companion bird/companion birds..1
   2, 7, 9, 19, 22, 32, 61, 64, 98, 100, 101, 107, 108, 109, 114, 142, 162
crop...2, 106, 163
cuttlebone..2

D

de-chlorinated water...73, 124
Diarrhea..101, 102
diet/diets..13, 37, 69, 70, 74, 88, 101, 124, 138, 147
disinfectants...62, 123
doxycycline...101

E

eggs...16, 17, 18, 131, 133
European Association of Avian Veterinarians...112
eye pinning..95

F

Feather plucking...91, 102, 103, 139, 149
feathers............. 2, 15, 28, 32, 33, 61, 77, 87, 92, 94, 95, 98, 101, 102, 106, 163, 164, 165
feces...73, 105, 106, 123
females..16, 33, 131
free flight..1, 49, 66, 74, 123, 129, 150
free flying..2
fruit/fruits...37, 38, 63, 69, 70, 71, 72, 125

G

Green–Winged Macaw..15
grooming...38, 77, 78, 127

Index

H

H5N1 .... 108, 109
habitat 1, 11, 12, 59, 60, 62, 74, 75, 83, 85, 122, 162
harness/harnesses 37, 85, 86, 128
hatchlings 18
health 3, 22, 32, 34, 38, 62, 97, 98, 100, 101, 109, 114, 116, 117, 118, 119, 134, 149
health problems 119, 138
HEPA filters 107
household chemicals 63, 123

I

illegal trade 12
insecticides 72
International Union for Conservation of Nature (IUCN) 12

J

Juvenile Scarlet Macaws 15

L

Leg disease 104
lifespan 137, 143
longevity 6, 18, 50, 103

M

males 18, 32, 33, 131
mineral block 37, 74, 127

N

nail clipping 78

Index

nests 12, 17, 18
North American Parrot Society 9, 10, 30, 89
nutrition 70, 124

O

outdoor aviary 26
outdoor enclosure 1, 64

P

Pacheco's disease 105, 106
Parrot Society of the UK 9, 30, 89
pellet/pellets 37, 69, 70, 72, 124, 147
perch/perches 16, 25, 59, 60, 63, 66, 67, 78, 79, 84, 85, 95, 103, 104, 122
pet insurance 39, 114, 117, 118, 119, 120
plumage 2, 94
preen 17, 94
Proventricular dilation disease 106

S

Scaly face 104
seeds 1, 13, 15, 69, 70, 72, 73, 124, 125, 147, 162
sexual maturity 16, 131, 163
shopping 58, 69, 119, 152
sleep 17, 75, 76, 150
speech 2, 80, 81, 148, 164
stainless steel cage 37, 61, 122

T

tail flaring 95
tails 14
toxic 13, 55, 56, 62, 63, 74, 78, 123
toys 24, 38, 63, 66, 67, 74, 75, 83, 90
travel carrier/travel crate 37, 64, 86, 87, 128

Index

tricks 5, 80, 82, 128, 148, 149

V

vegetables 37, 38, 63, 69, 71, 72, 125, 147
Vet Index Directory 112
veterinarian/veterinarians 2, 3, 22, 78, 105, 109, 110, 112, 113, 114, 120, 127, 162
vinegar 62, 123
vitamin/vitamins 61, 73, 147
vocabulary 80, 148

W

water 27, 37, 53, 60, 62, 63, 72, 73, 77, 78, 87, 93, 105, 123, 124, 127, 150
wing clipping 28, 29
wing flapping 95
wings 2, 15, 28, 51, 77, 78, 95, 106

Z

zoonotic 3, 22, 100, 108, 165

Photo Credits

Cover Design:– Liliana Gonzalez Garcia, www.ipublicidades.com (info@ipublicidades.com)

Photo by Bohemianism
http://www.flickr.com/photos/bohemianism/4250130647/sizes/m/

Photo by I, Snowmanradio via Wikimedia Commons
http://commons.wikimedia.org/wiki/File%3AScarlet_macaw_eating_31107.JPG

Photo Credits

Photo by César Rincón (originally posted to Flickr as 20050404113105–0), via Wikimedia Commons
http://commons.wikimedia.org/wiki/File%3AScarlet_Macaw_(Ara_macao)_–two_on_perch.jpg

Photo by Mohd Nor Azmil Abdul Rahman (originally posted to Flickr as Red Red Wine via Wikimedia Commons
http://commons.wikimedia.org/wiki/File%3AScarlet_Macaw_(Ara_macao).jpg

Photo by Travis Isaacs from Grapevine, TX, USA (zoo355 Uploaded by snowmanradio) via Wikimedia Commons
http://commons.wikimedia.org/wiki/File%3AAra_macao_–Fort_Worth_Zoo–8.jpg

Photo Credits

Photo by TJL23
http://www.flickr.com/photos/36718407@N00/243545485/sizes/m/

Photo by Adalberto H Vega
http://www.flickr.com/photos/ahvega/3682631417/sizes/m/

Photo by © Copyright Oast House Archive and licensed for reuse under this Creative Commons Licence
http://www.geograph.org.uk/photo/1202428

Photo by Loren Sztager
http://www.flickr.com/photos/lorensztajer/4201256040/sizes/l/

Photo Credits

Photo by Carolina Lopez (originally posted to Flickr as Guacamaya traviesa), via Wikimedia Commons
https://commons.wikimedia.org/wiki/File%3AScarlet_Macaw_%28Ara_macao%29_-chewing_wood.jpg

Photo by Adalberto H. Vega
http://www.flickr.com/photos/ahvega/3683443448/sizes/o/

Photo by Dick Daniels (http://carolinabirds.org/) (Own work) via Wikimedia Commons
http://commons.wikimedia.org/wiki/File%3AScarlet_Macaw_(Ara_macao)_RWD.jpg

Photo Credits

Photo by Jar0d, via Wikimedia Commons
http://commons.wikimedia.org/wiki/File%3AAra_macao_-Diergaarde_Blijdorp_-flying-8a.jpg

Photo by Adalberto H Vega
http://www.flickr.com/photos/ahvega/3682644077/sizes/m/

Photo by en:User:Cburnett (Own work), via Wikimedia Commons
http://commons.wikimedia.org/wiki/File%3AScarlet_Macaw.jpg

Photo Credits

Photo by Loren Sztager
http://www.flickr.com/photos/lorensztajer/4611915409/sizes/m/

All Creative Commons work

These works are licensed under the Creative Commons Attribution 3.0 Unported License. To view a copy of this license, visit http://creativecommons.org/licenses/by/3.0/ or send a letter to Creative Commons, 444 Castro Street, Suite 900, Mountain View, California, 94041, USA.

Photo courtesy www.tropicalbirdshop.com

Photo Credits

All other photos – www.bigstockphotos.com